BERNINA®

SEWING LUXURIOUS PILLOWS

Artistic Designs for Home Decor

BERNINA®

SEWING LUXURIOUS PILLOWS

Artistic Designs for Home Decor

Linda Lee

The Bernina Sewing Library

Sewing Information Resources, Wasco, IL

Sewing Information Resources
P.O. Box 330
Wasco, Illinois 60183

Sewing Information Resources is a registered trademark of Ganz Inc.
Editor: JoAnn Pugh-Gannon
Photography: Nathan Ham Photography, Topeka, KS
Electonic page layout and design: Ernie Shelton, Shelton Design Studios
Index: Anne Leach

Printed in Hong Kong.
ISBN: 1-886884-08-0

Linda Lee, ASID, IIDA, is a licensed interior designer and has owned her own residential and commercial design firm since 1974. She owns The Sewing Workshop, a sewing school in San Francisco, specializing in classes for all levels of sewing, fitting, embellishment, fine craft, and textile arts. In addition, she is the owner of Threadwear, an upscale fabric store in Topeka, Kansas. Utilizing her many talents, Linda produces a boutique line of contemporary clothing patterns and is a contributing editor of <u>Threads</u> magazine, as well as a contributing writer to <u>Sewing Today Newsletter</u>. She was also senior editor for the <u>Vogue/Butterick Designer Sewing Techniques</u> book and a content editor and scriptwriter for the PBS sewing series, <u>Sewing Today</u>.

DEDICATION

This book is dedicated to my mother, the English teacher, and my father, the printer, who valued the written word and taught me to appreciate a beautiful printed page.

Alexandra, my 7-year-old creative daughter, drew the best pillow designs of all. Thanks to Alex and Craig for allowing me the space and energy to put forth the effort.

And thanks to my friend, Marcy Tilton, for giving me the opportunity to own The Sewing Workshop, the premier sewing school she founded, which in turn opened the door for me.

TABLE OF CONTENTS

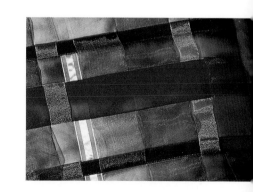

INTRODUCTION

Pillows add character to an interior space. They can be functional or beautiful or both. But mostly they can express an idea of a feeling about you or how you want to live without a major investment of time and money. This book is a beauty book of pillow ideas. It has the added feature of being a technique book for people who like to sew. Here is an opportunity to experiment with sewing techniques, become familiar with sewing equipment and accessories, and play with fabrics and trims in a creative process without having to measure your waistline. So, it is a teaching tool, in a sense, for techniques that may be incorporated later into art-to-wear garment construction, additional home decorating projects or fine crafts.

The information in this chapter is basic in the construction of most pillows and especially in the construction of the projects in this book. As the other chapters feature singular artistic details relating to the individual projects, this chapter reviews techniques that are **Chapter 1** germane to common pillow-making.

11

NOTIONS AND TOOLS

I love notions and tools. I think I love them more than fabric, which is pretty hard to believe, but having the right tools and equipment is as important as knowing the techniques. I have spent my sewing lifetime gathering things, testing them, rejecting them, and always trying new gadgets. The recommendations throughout this book for notions and equipment are not tossed out lightly. I believe that if you use them, your sewing will improve. Buy a few at a time, put them on your Christmas list, save your money for them. You will be glad you did. Here are a few of my favorites.

The Sewing Machine

My sewing machine is my best friend. I don't own the absolute latest model with all the fancy stitches, but I certainly own a very new, computerized model with a lot of options. And the most important feature of this machine is that it makes a beautiful stitch. It comes with a few presser feet and I have purchased every other presser foot available. It's sturdy. It's beautifully designed. It cost a lot of money, and it is set up in my sewing room all of the time.

I oil it regularly. I dust it once a week. I change needles on every project. I use good-quality cotton thread, and I have it serviced once a year. In the 35 years that I've been sewing, I have never had a breakdown.

The Serger

My serger is primarily a finishing tool. I wouldn't want to live without it, but I could in a pinch. Unless you are seriously into quick-and-easy serging projects sewn exclusively on a serger, my recommendation is to buy a major European brand, 4-thread serger with differential feed.

Scissors and Rotary Cutter

As you can see from the photo at the beginning of this chapter, I own practically every scissors made. However, I don't always cut out a project with scissors. In fact, I always try my rotary cutter first. But, scissors perform other great functions — trimming, clipping, grading, snipping and pinking. No one pair of scissors can do it all. I recently treated myself to a pair of handmade Japanese dressmaker's shears. They cut through a piece of fabric like butter and now all I want to do is cut with them. Find the best scissors that work for you.

Pins

I have a thing about pins. When I am teaching classes, I am always amazed at the pitiful assortment of pins that most students have. They're either bent, minuscule, or as big as nails. Find the best imported glass head silk pins. They are a pure pleasure to use. And replace them often. By the way, a magnetic pin cushion for holding your pins is the best invention in recent times.

Clear Rulers

As an interior designer, I have worked with many kinds of good-quality architectural drafting rulers. So, I've gotten spoiled. For sewing, I use 1"-, 2"-, and 3"-wide, clear plastic rulers that have grids on them in 1/8" increments. I do a lot of trimming and cutting using these rulers and a rotary cutter, and I think that my sewing is more precise as a result.

Seam Ripper

Most people dislike ripping. I actually like to rip. But of course, I have the ultimate ripper and it makes short work of this process. Buy the best Japanese-made ripper you can find with the finest and sharpest point and cutting edge.

Markers

A small, consistent fine line of chalk is essential when sewing. I like the fact that this line stays for the duration of the sewing process, but it will brush away easily. Chalk markers are available in several shapes and generally can be refilled in one of several colors. White and blue are my favorites. Red won't always come out of the fabric.

Needles

I keep a large supply of sewing machine and hand-sewing needles on hand. I remember the days when I changed needles in my sewing machine when one broke. Now I change a needle after every project and/or when I change fabric or sewing technique. The finer the fabric, the smaller the needle size used; the heavier the fabric or number of layers, the larger the needle. There are specialty needles for sewing with metallic thread to avoid fraying, for sewing leather and suede, and for sewing with microfibers and many other types of fabrics or threads. Whenever your sewing machine is misbehaving, try changing the needle and rethreading first, before going into an utter state of panic about the condition of your machine.

TECHNIQUES FOR SEWING PILLOWS
Sewing Corners

Most pillows have right-angled corners. They seem simple enough to sew, but there are a few tips to avoid "dog-eared" corners.

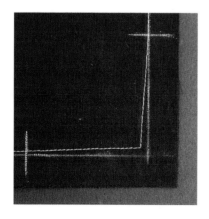

Using a chalk marker, draw a 1/2" seam allowance along each corner. In the interior sewing industry, seam allowances are 1/2" wide. Begin sewing the pillow sections together. Approximately 2" from the corner, begin tapering the stitching to the inside increasing the overall seam allowance at the corner to approximately 5/8" or 3/4". Pivot. Taper back out to the 1/2" seam allowance on the other side of the corner. Trim the excess fabric across the point.

When sewing a corner in a box pillow, stitch to the exact point, insert the needle into the fabric and clip the boxing fabric to the point. Pivot the fabric, align the raw edges again and continue to sew.

Pillow Closures

There are five methods of enclosing a pillow:

slip-stitching,

zippers,

overlapping edges,

Velcro™, or

buttons or snaps.

Today, professional workrooms rarely use zippers in decorative pillows. Slip-stitching an opening by hand is the most concealed method of closing a pillow cover. Overlapping edges, buttoning and Velcro™ are the most common. These methods allow easy removal of the covers for cleaning and rejuvenation. These closures can also be integrated into the overall design of the pillow itself.

To prepare the hemmed edges for either overlap, button, or Velcro™ closures, cut a 2" X 10" piece of oak tag as a template. Now is a good opportunity to practice using a clear ruler and a rotary cutter. Place the template approximately 2" from the raw edge of the fabric and press the fabric up and over the template, aligning the raw edge of the fabric with the top of the template.

Prepare a 1 1/2" X 10" oak tag template. Place the template in the well of the pressed crease and press 1/2" up and over the bottom edge of the template. Topstitch next to the inner fold.

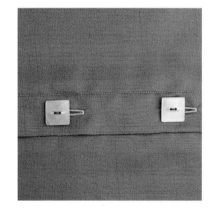

A button closure is both functional and attractive. Prepare the overlap and underlying piece using hem templates. Make buttonholes on the overlap all the same size using the automatic buttonhole selection on the machine. Sew buttons to the bottom layer. Button closures can appear on either the front or back of a pillow.

Sewing Velcro™ strips to the overlap and underlay is the most secure method of closing a pillow while still allowing for flexibility. I found Velcro™ to be too heavy for most light- to mid-weight fabrics. Save this method of closure for industrial strength projects.

I was first introduced to the idea of using templates from several teachers at The Sewing Workshop in San Francisco. Shermane Fouché taught me to cut a pocket shape to use as a pressing tool. David Coffin of <u>Threads</u> magazine showed me how to cut a template for a perfect sleeve placket. And Marcy Tilton passed along the technique of cutting strips of oak tag to use as pressing tools for hems. This is one of those tips that you will not realize is so good until you try it. You'll get hooked.

Piping and Cording

Certain styles of pillows and fabrics look more professional when outlined with a cord or corded piping. Learn to make your own corded piping or purchase decorative twisted cord for the edge.

TERMS:

piping - a flat, narrow fabric or braid used to finish raw edges on material

cord - plies of yarns that have been twisted together to form a single strand used as filler

corded piping - a bias strip of fabric with a cord inserted into the center

tubing - woven or knitted fabric in a cylindrical form

welting - a fabric-covered cord sewn on a seam or used as a border

flange - a projecting rim or extension to the cord or corded piping

MAKING PIPING, CORDING, AND FILLED TUBING

Making your own corded piping takes a little practice, and there are a few tricks that will help make it easier. The right materials, the right presser feet, and the right finishing techniques will get you on your way.

MATERIALS NEEDED:

- fabric
- filler — cotton cable cord in medium to very large or rattail cord for very small
- mitered clear ruler
- 2"- or 3"-wide gridded clear ruler
- rotary cutter and cutting mat
- fine-line chalk marker
- 3-groove or 5-groove pintuck presser foot for fine cording
- cording foot for medium cording
- leather roller foot for oversized cording

Even though it requires more fabric, corded piping is easier to maneuver when the fabric strips that are used to wrap the filler are cut on the bias. Sometimes you may not have enough fabric, so it is acceptable to use fabric that has been cut on the crosswise or lengthwise grain.

The special presser feet described in this section are important. Using these feet allows you to get closer to the inner cord thereby getting a tighter and more even corded piping. For years, I used a regular zipper foot, but I disliked making corded piping because it never really looked good when I was done. The various presser feet listed on page 17 made the difference for me. Now I sew trims with confidence.

To cut strips of fabric on the bias, it is useful to invest in a clear ruler that has a 45° diagonal edge or cut out your fabric on a cutting mat that has a 45° line drawn on it. Square up your fabric on the table and use either the diagonal ruler edge or the mat lines to cut the first bias line. Each consecutive cutting line can be marked with a straight edge and chalk marker. I find that using either method produces the most precise cutting line.

Chances are you will need multiple strips of fabric since most fabrics are too narrow to give you a long enough bias for one pillow. To join strips in a continuous bias, place two strips right sides together at right angles to each other. Align the actual 1/4" seam allowance stitching lines and sew. Press the seam allowances open. The resulting diagonal seam is less obvious on corded piping and is less bulky.

When making **medium-sized corded piping**, wrap the bias strip around cotton cable cord with the wrong sides together and feed through a presser foot called a bulky overlock foot. This foot has a groove on the underside that allows the cord to travel through the foot evenly and stabilizes it while you sew. Move the needle position on your sewing machine all the way to the right.

To make **small corded piping**, repeat the same process as above, but this time the filler is a small, tubular trim called rattail cord, and the presser foot is a 3-groove pintuck foot. One of the grooves on the presser foot is the exact size of rattail cord. I like to use the center groove and change the needle position to the right. Rattail cord is readily available, sold by the yard, and comes in many beautiful colors. The smallest diameter of rattail or cotton cable cord fits into a single groove of a 5-groove foot.

Oversized corded piping is especially popular these days, and sewing it requires a very unique piece of equipment. A presser foot called a leather roller foot has a very large wheel that actually moves the fabric along.

The jumbo corded piping may be left plain or it can be shirred as you sew. After sewing for several inches, hold onto the fabric behind the presser foot with one hand and pull the cable cord in front of the presser foot with the other. Work the fabric to spread the shirring evenly.

Sometimes you will want to embellish the surface of a piece with **filled tubing**, and in this case, a flange is unnecessary. Even though there are lots of new and improved turning devices to aid in making filled tubing, I find that most often I use the classic method that I learned from a friend who has sewn for over 60 years.

To make self-filled tubing, cut a strip of fabric four times the width of the finished tubing. Cut a piece of pearl cotton longer than the bias strip. Tie a large knot at one end. Fold the bias strip in half lengthwise with right sides together. Insert the knotted pearl cotton inside next to the fold with the knot extending out the top of the fabric. Begin stitching at the top, backstitching over the pearl cotton, and tapering out to the exact center of the strip. Stitch the entire length of the strip.

Trim the fabric around the backstitching. Hold the pearl cotton in one hand, begin to pull, and gently ease the knotted end into the tube. Continue to pull the cord completely through itself until you have a long length of self-filled tubing. The finished tubing can be handsewn or sewn by machine with the blindstitch to any surface.

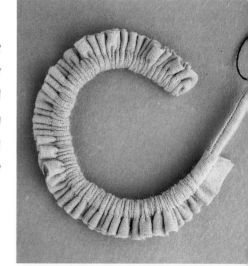

MAKING FLANGED TRIMS

A variety of trims are readily available in most sewing and home decorating stores. Look for trims with flanges that can be sewn directly into a seam, beautiful twisted cords without flanges, and unique novelty fringes.

Inevitably, the right color combination you need just cannot be found. Now there is a way to create your own twisted cord trim in custom colors using an interesting piece of equipment resembling a fishing reel called the spinster. Check the Resource List for more information.

Combine six to eight strands of exotic yarns and threads. Tie one end of the group to a door knob or a chair leg. Tie a loop at the other end and place it over the hook of the spinster. As you wind the reel, the yarns twist. Keep twisting them tightly.

While keeping the twisted cord stretched, remove the cord from the tool and place a pencil through the loop. Grasp the pencil with one hand and hold the center of the strand with the other hand. Insert the pencil through the end tied to the door knob or chair.

Slowly release the strands a few inches at a time so that the two cords twist together and become one cord. Remove the cord from the door knob or chair leg and tie the ends together.

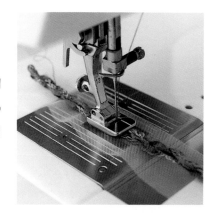

By sewing a strip of Seams Great™ to the twisted cord, you add a flange to the trim making it easy to sew into a seam or edge. Use a blindstitch foot and the corresponding blindstitch setting.

To insert a flanged cord into a seam, align the raw edge of the pillow front with the outer edge of the flange and pin in place. Select a bulky overlock foot, change the needle position to the far right and stitch in place. Clip the flange at the corner to allow it to spread and lie flat.

With right sides together, pin the pillow back to the front, sandwiching the cord between the layers. Use the same foot, move the needle position closer to the cording and stitch. Trim the corners and turn the pillow inside out.

FINISHING THE ENDS

Corded piping and twisted cord need to be finished nicely to conceal the raw edges. With a little practice, all evidence of joining these trims will be hidden.

When using fabric-covered corded piping, begin stitching the trim about 1 1/2" from the end along the pillow edge. Continue around all sides of the pillow. About 1 1/2" from the other end of the trim, stop stitching and leave the needle in the fabric. Remove a few stitches from the corded piping and push the fabric back to expose the cable cord. Trim the cord so that it just touches the other cord end.

Fold under the raw edge of the bias strip of fabric. Slip the bias strip around the adjoining cording, and continue to stitch the trim in place.

Twisted cord with a flange is sewn to a pillow in the same way as corded piping. To finish the ends properly, leave about 1 1/2" of cord and flange not sewn along the pillow edge with 3" tails at either end. Cut away the flange from the tails, un-twist the strands, and wrap tape around each strand. Overlap the remaining ends of the flange and tape down. Place the right-hand group of strands facing up and the left-hand group facing down.

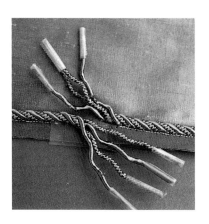

Thread the right-hand group of strands under the taped flange and twist them back into their original order. Tape in place.

Lay the left-hand group of strands over the right-hand group, twisting and arranging them until they also are back to their original configuration and the cord looks like one continuous strand.

Chapter 1

Continue to stitch the cording to the pillow edge and trim any extra strands.

Decorative Flanges and Fringes

As rims and extensions — from flat to fluffy — flanges and fringes outline pillows and give them definition. Sometimes they are subtle and integral to the overall pillow design. But many times, they are the primary design feature adorning a pillow.

A **simple flange** is a piece of fabric folded lengthwise, wrong sides together, and sandwiched between the top and bottom layers of the pillow.

The same type of flange can be padded up with one or more layers of cotton batting placed inside the folded flange.

An extension does not have to be sewn onto the pillow to be considered a flange. The pillow pieces, themselves, can be cut larger to include the flange. The flange of this metallic sheer pillow is defined by a hand-stitched row of decorative rayon thread. The inner pillow is China silk. Vintage metal rosettes embellish the corners.

Another type of flange is the **ruffle**. There are a number of ways to make ruffles, but a ruffler attachment makes precise ruffles that are easy to sew and attach to another surface. A ruffler accessory for a sewing machine is quite an investment, but for home decorating projects that involve making extra-long ruffled sections, it no longer becomes a luxury to own one.

I call this **designer fringe** because you can buy this fabulous fringe through the interior design trade for an exorbitant price, or you can make a perfect look-alike for a fraction of the designer price. Here's how.

You'll need enough 1"-wide grosgrain ribbon to go around the pillow edges and one yard of rayon seam tape for every 2" of finished fringe. Just any rayon seam tape will not do. Purchase the tape that is packaged on a roll and is sold by the yard. See the Resource List for more information.

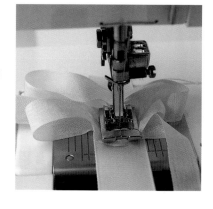

Center the grosgrain ribbon under the presser foot. Working from side to side, crisscross, fold, stack and twist the rayon tape and stitch it to the ribbon.

Vary the lengths of the loops, long to short. It is not necessary to be neat and consistent with this process. One side of the loops can be trimmed so that there is less bulk inserted into the seam. Or only the ribbon can be inserted into the seam and all the lengths of loops left exposed, creating two layers.

Another interesting fringe, called caterpillar fringe, uses multiple strands of mixed yarns and threads wrapped around a section of a coat hanger. I learned this technique from Helen Saunders, a wonderful fiber artist from Boulder, Colorado.

To make a fringe hook, cut a section of coat hanger with wire cutters and file the cut ends smooth. Bend the hanger to form a deep "U". The length of the finished fringe will equal one-half of the distance between the wires forming the "U".

Cut a piece of fabric, such as a lightweight faux suede, 2" wide. Center the strip under the presser foot. Wind a mixture of yarns and threads around the fringe hook and stitch through the center of the fibers. Pull the hook forward, wrap more yarns, and continue to stitch.

Remove the strip from the sewing machine and cut the loops on both sides.

Fold the fabric strip in half lengthwise, doubling the fringe, and creating a flange to sew into the seam. Pin the strip to the edges of the pillow and sew close to the fringe.

To insert the fringe in a seam, place the corresponding pillow section on top of the fringe and sew over the previous stitching through all the layers.

Decorative Corner Treatments

Turkish, tasseled, tied and trimmed — pillow corners are the frosting and candles of pillow-making.

TURKISH CORNER

A Turkish corner is a soft corner formed by pleating the fabric before sewing the pillow sections together.

With right sides together, fold the fabric, matching the raw edges and creating a diagonal fold. Place a pin about 1 1/2" from the corner.

Keeping the first pin in place, flatten the corner of the fabric evenly and pin on both sides of the first pin. Repeat this step for all four corners of both the front and back for a total of eight times. As you sew the front and back sections together, stitch the corners slightly curved. Small inverted tucks will show on the outside of the pillow on either side of the seam.

TASSELED CORNERS

A unique way to add a tassel to a corner is to loop it through a decorative cord, allowing the loop to become part of the corner detail.

Cut away 1/2" of the seam allowance at each corner.

Sew the corded piping to the edge of the pillow in the usual manner. Continue stitching the corners where the flange has been removed.

After you have sewn the pillow sections together, the section of corded piping that does not have the flange will be floating to which a tassel can be tied.

KNOTTED CORNERS

This tied knot is simply an 18" square of crinkled China silk. Using silk thread and a 3-thread stitch formation on a serger, roll-hem the edges of the squares. Tie each square in a single knot. As the corner of the pillow is sewn, part of the knot is caught in the stitching.

MAKING TASSELS

With the explosion of trims available for interior accessories, there is a profusion of great tassels on the market today. But unfortunately, they are likely to be expensive or the color combination is not suitable for the project. Consider making your own tassel using luxurious yarns.

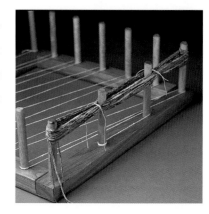

To make a finished 9" tassel, you will need to find two stationary objects that are 18" apart. Objects such as chair legs, C-clamps or door knobs are fine, but a warping board is perfect. Wrap at least eight strands of yarn around two pegs. The number of times you wrap them determines the fullness of the tassel. When the wrapping is complete, tie the strands together in two places with crochet cotton.

Remove the strands from the warping board pegs. Tie crochet cotton around the strands at the center, 9" from each end. Cut the loop ends.

Using an 8" piece of twisted cord, like that used in making the decorative piping above, tie a simple overhand knot in the center and pull snugly. Just above that knot, tie another knot, leaving a 1/2" space between.

Lay the center of the strands under the cord and above both knots. Bring the strands over the cord. Wrap a piece of crochet cotton around all strands and between the knots. Remove the other ties and let the yarns cascade. With a toothpick, place one drop of water on the knot to set it.[1]

Wrap a double strand of matching yarn around the crochet cotton tie. Thread the strand through a very large needle or bodkin and hide the end of the yarns by stabbing the needle through the first knot. Now that the twisted cord is on the center of the tassel, cut the ends and untwist the cord to get the individual strands to blend with the finsihed tassel.

Feed the exposed portion of the twisted cord through the corner of the pillow and tie a large knot on the inside. Stitch the corner as usual.

Allow the tassel to hang freely and "comb" it, trimming the ends.

Three colors of silk chenille yarn were used to make these 9" tassels which adorn an oversized printed silk velvet pillow.

Texture. Of all the basic design elements, texture may be the most intriguing. Tactile sensations bring interesting associations from the far-reaching depths of our minds and bodies. The surface of a pillow is a canvas just waiting for your **Chapter 2** own personal statement — a chance to experiment with texture in many forms, a study in what feels good.

SURFACE DESIGN

SURFACE DESIGN

REVERSE APPLIQUÉ

Reverse appliqué is a method of creating dimensional textures by overlapping pieces of fabric, stitching them together, and trimming layers away to expose secondary fabrics, designs, and colors.

Working with washed wool is Jean Cacicedo's specialty. This San Francisco designer began as a painter, became interested in macramé, and then settled on working with wool fabric as a means of her expression. She didn't invent reverse appliqué, but she developed the technique of washing varieties of wool coating, wool jersey, and any other fabric that softens and changes texture when washed. She uses this "new" art-to-wear clothing combining abstract patterns and colors.

Jean throws any wool fabric into the washing machine. The results can be a complete surprise or there may be no change at all. She has even been known to wash a piece of fabric as many as twenty times to get the result she wants. She also has a good understanding of ordinary washing machine dyes.

I asked her to shift her attention to a pillow shape instead of a human body, and she obliged.

Chapter 2

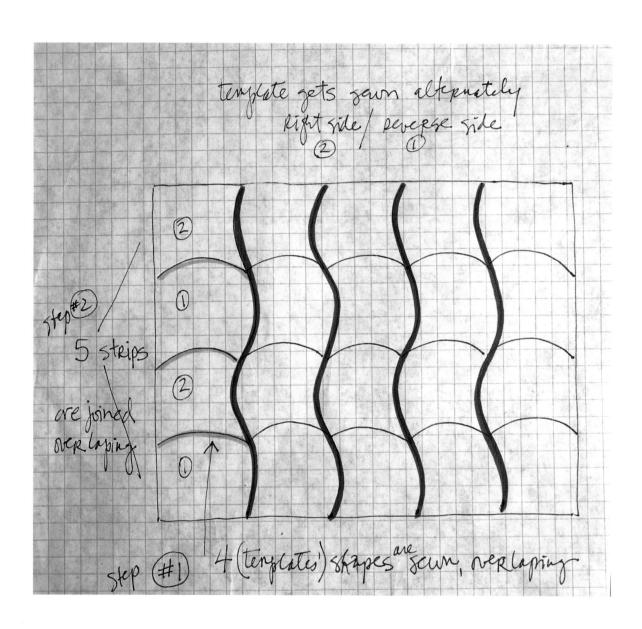

Planning a design on paper first is essential. Draw a design at quarter scale by using graph paper with 1/4" squares that represent 1". To make templates of each different shape, enlarge the pattern, draw it again on oak tag, and cut out the template.

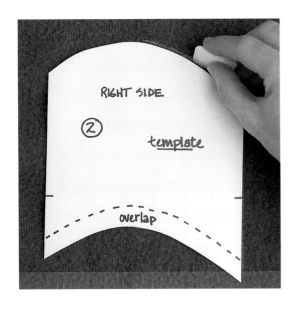

Place the template on the right side of the fabric and trace around it. On fabrics with a dense pile, a wax marker shows well. Part of the planning of the design is to determine which pieces overlap others. The piece on top does not need to have a seam allowance added. Add seam allowances to the underlying pieces.

After the fabric pieces have been cut out, overlap the appropriate sections and straight-stitch close to the raw edge. Place a second row of topstitching about 1/4" from the first.

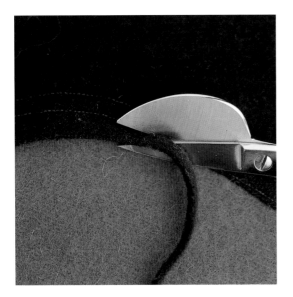

On the wrong side, trim the excess fabric close to the second row of stitching. Appliqué scissors make quick work of trimming and hinder any cutting mistakes. After wool fabrics have been washed a few times, the edges do not ravel.

SURFACE DESIGN

Jennie Atwood works in a similar media. Her garden vegetables on a black background have a quaint folk art influence, and the designs are borrowed from traditional appliqué patterns.

A clever but simple way to close this pillow is to trim the edges with pinking shears or use a pinked-edge rotary cutter. Overlap the back pieces and use a strip of steamed and rolled wool jersey to sew the edges closed with a jumbo running stitch.

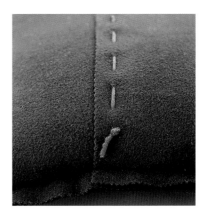

Chapter 2

WINDOWPANE FABRIC

My associate, Stephanie Valley, made a vest using wool flannel with cut-out squares exposing a layer of silk organza. I wore that vest everywhere, and it was a sensation.

The technique can be adapted to include opaque treatments; thus the inspiration for this pillow made from Ultrasuede™ and striped silk douppioni.

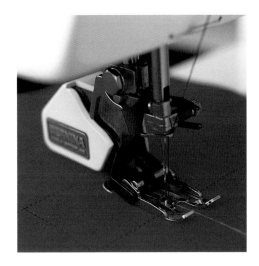

Place the two layers of fabric together so that the right side of the bottom layer will show when the top layer is cut away. Using a chalk marker, draw the pattern on the top layer. Stitch the two layers together, using the markings as a guide. When sewing on Ultrasuede™ or other faux suedes, use a walking foot to prevent the fabric from creeping and to keep the work flat.

Using sharp, pointed trimming scissors of good quality, cut away portions of the top layer to expose the striped layer below. Cut the stripe on the bias so that the pattern runs diagonally through the "windows."

Vary the cut-out shapes for added interest. Choose squares, diamonds, triangles, and other custom shapes.

Chapter 2

SMOCKING AND SHIRRING

Shirring is a traditional sewing term for drawing up or gathering fabric on three or more parallel threads. It is most often referred to as smocking on children's clothing and vintage costumes. Using this technique as the surface of a pillow is a more contemporary approach.

The finer the fabric the more textured the shirring becomes. Choose a drapey, silk novelty weave for the pillow shirring and then edge it with a crisp silk douppioni ruffle.

This technique is achieved by using elastic thread in the bobbin and regular thread on top. Slightly loosen the tension on a extra bobbin case. Wind the elastic thread onto a bobbin. Mark parallel lines on the fabric as stitching guides. Elongate the stitch length to at least 4mm, and sew multiple rows of straight stitches. The final step is to hold an iron over the fabric and steam the rows of stitching. The elastic will draw up even more.

Another form of shirring is inspired by the work of Ana Lisa Hedstrom, a San Francisco designer. Ana Lisa has developed a technique of creating unexpected texture using a traditional smocking machine. The silk crepe de chine used on this pillow has an irregular, hand-dyed appearance.

This smocking machine has fine needles that are threaded with metallic thread. Thread every needle or leave some empty for a random texture.

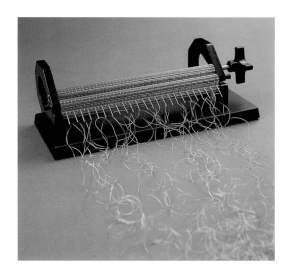

SURFACE DESIGN

The fabric is placed between the two rollers, similar to the old-fashioned wringer washing machine. By turning the rollers, the fabric feeds from front to back and the fabric is threaded at even intervals. After all the fabric has gone through the machine, the gathers can be manipulated to achieve interesting changes in texture from very compact to loose.

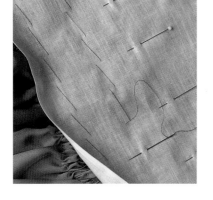

To keep the shirring in place, pin a fabric underlining, such as batiste, to the wrong side of the piece. Using silk thread, hand-baste the underlining with rows of long stitches. Finish stitching the pillow according to your design.

FRAGMENTS AND PIECES

Collecting bits and pieces of vintage fabric, tapestry, needlepoint, and trims is a life-long passion for many people. Antique stores, flea markets, resale shops, and small shops that specialize in rare finds are great resources for the odd and tempting piece. The sewing connoisseur buys freely without knowing when, where, or how something will be used.

An 18th-century tapestry bell cord was the starting point for this pillow. Add a piece of faded fringe, mix the companion fabrics, and you have the best of the new and the best of the old.

Chapter 2

A special presser foot with an uneven sole accommodating a flat piping on one side, eases the sewing process when stitching a band to another surface. This foot won't slide off of the band and create irregular edgestitching as would happen with the standard presser foot.

A vintage fringe commonly has a raised and twisted cord to finish an edge. To conceal the stitching, but durably attach this trim, use a presser foot that has a groove on the underside, such as a cording foot. Move the needle position to the right, center the cord under the groove, and stitch.

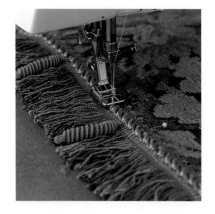

Little pieces of beautiful textiles to incorporate into pillows can be found on dresses from resale shops or in grandmother's attic. Usually the shape of the remnant will dictate how it is used in the overall design. Let the piece inspire you, and don't use it until it does.

The featured fabric on this pillow is a silk sash found in an old dresser. The snaps and hooks were removed, and the silk was carefully laundered and pressed.

Some fabrics are delicate and need to be backed and quilted. Sandwich a piece of cotton batting between the sash and a backing fabric. Pin all the layers together at intervals. Some presser feet can accommodate a calibrated quilt guide which allows parallel stitching with ease. Mark the first row of stitching and let the stitching guide do the rest of the work.

Tubing can be attached to an edge with a special stitch and presser foot. Select an edgestitch foot, mirror the blindstitch direction, and place the guide between the pillow edge and the tubing. Set the needle position so that the straight stitch portion of the blindstitch sews along the edge of the fabric, and the zigzag stitch slightly catches the tubing. Use monofilament thread for invisible stitches.

Chapter 2

One of the advantages of using a blindstitch to apply tubing to an edge is that parts of the tubing can remain loose to allow for a corner knot.

A metallic gold mesh collar (a flea market find!) embellishes this black, rayon velvet pillow.

The collar is very heavy, so it requires stabilizing. Underline the velvet with double-sided cotton flannel and hand-baste the collar to both layers.

An old chair may be useless, but the upholstery may be worth keeping, especially if it is a piece
of needlepoint in good condition. Cut around the general needlepoint shape and mount it on
iridescent taffeta. Trim the edge with a double layer of muted gold antique fringe.

SURFACE DESIGN

An old needlepoint technique used canvas over velveteen. Each needlepoint stitch went through both layers of fabric. Clean up the piece by trimming any excess canvas and removing unfinished or unnecessary yarn and stitches.

Place the needlepointed velveteen on the background. Use an ordinary dinner plate to draw a gentle curving shape around the needlepoint. Straight-stitch the velveteen to the background along the marked line. Using appliqué scissors, carefully trim the excess velveteen close to the stitching.

Use an antique gold flat braid to cover the raw edge of the velveteen. Move the needle position to the right, attach an edgestitch foot, and stitch along the outside edge of the trim.

You may need to "build" a more substantial trim to enhance the needlepoint or to complement the scale with the overall piece. Apply a matching metallic cord centered on the top of the flat braid. A presser foot that is traditionally used for pintucking can be used as a cording foot. Use the center groove of a five-groove pintuck foot to hold the small decorative cord while couching it with a narrow zigzag stitch.

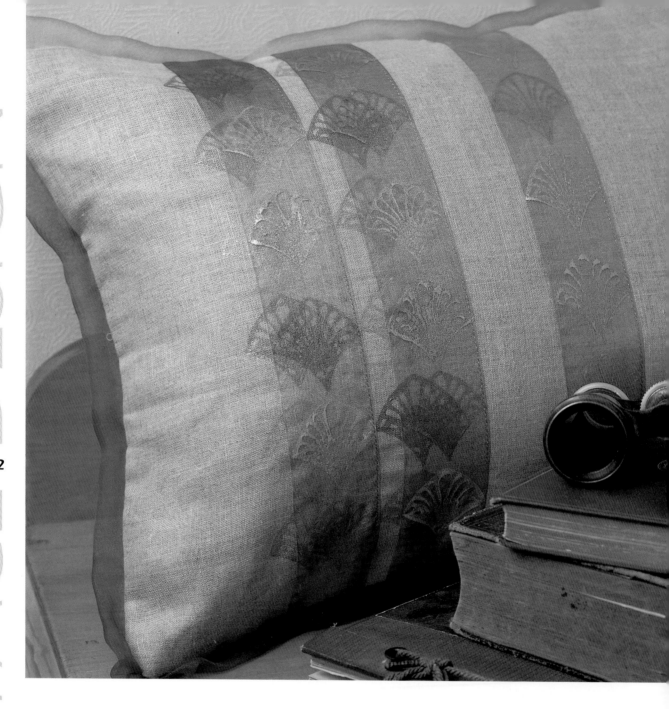

STAMPED AND STITCHED

With the popularity of rubber stamping on paper, it is only natural to assume that stamping on fabric was next to come. With a little persistence, rubber stamps designed for fabric are available by mail order and in some art supply stores. Fabric stamps have a broader surface and are not as finely detailed as paper stamps.

One stamp motif is used on this pillow and repeated many times. Four colors of metallic fabric paint have been stamped in a vertical pattern on linen and repeated on sheer and variegated ribbon. When stamping on sheer ribbon, place plain paper under the ribbon to control the bleed-through.

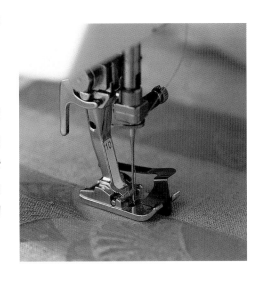

Place the ribbon overlays slightly to the side of the identical design on the linen for a shadow effect. Using metallic sewing thread, stitch on one side of the ribbon only. Remember to use a special sewing needle called a Metalfil needle when sewing with metallic thread. This needle prevents thread breakage and tangles.

The supplies needed to produce this stamped and stitched pillow are fabric stamps, either purchased or cut from thin cork and mounted on cardboard; good-quality metallic fabric paints, such as Lumiere; foam brushes; sheer ribbon; fabric; and metallic thread.

LAYERED SHEERS

Interesting things happen when you layer an iridescent chiffon over a China silk fabric. Experiment with different colors of China silk as the color changes are dramatic.

Chapter 2

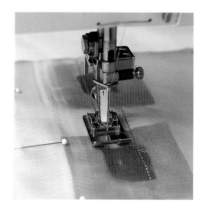

Cut or tear two sizes of small squares of metallic sheers. Develop a checkerboard pattern by placing small squares over larger squares and sandwich them between the chiffon and China silk layers. Again, using metallic thread in a Metalfil needle, stitch parallel lines through all four layers. Embellish the surface with thread, beads, and baubles.

BUTTON FLOWERS

Fashion and button designer Todd Oldham designed a jacket adorned with hundreds of buttons. The button jacket was the inspiration for this button pillow. The pillow weighs a ton, but I love the way it looks like candy and is even a little bit noisy!

The buttons are not as randomly placed as it may seem at first glance. There is a central button surrounded by a group of identical buttons, forming clusters of circular floral shapes. Ordinary buttons are enhanced by stacking other buttons on top, basic buttons are next to special buttons, and the colors are mixed.

Choose a sturdy background such as a colorful denim for the base fabric. Speed the button application process by using a button sew-on foot on the sewing machine. Temporarily adhere the buttons to the surface with a glue stick before permanently sewing the buttons in place.

The triangular flat flange on the button pillow is actually two pieces of fabric sewn together to form one complete piece. To get sharp points on the flange, use a presser foot designed to sew perfect 1/4" seams and turn corners at precisely 1/4" from the raw edges. Sew to the turning point, insert the needle into the fabric, lift the presser foot, pivot the fabric 90°, and continue stitching.

Turn the flange to the outside and press the edges. For crisper edges, first press the seams open over a point presser, then turn the work to the right side and press. Staystitch the inside corners along the 1/2" seam allowance and clip to the point. Don't be shy about this. The closer the clip to the corner stitch, the less chance for a pucker.

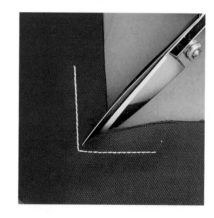

To apply the flange to the pillow, align the raw edges of the seam allowances with the flange towards the center of the pillow. Stitch perfect corners by following the staystitching line and pivoting at the clip.

NECKTIES REVISITED

Artist and pattern maker Angela Candela has developed a technique for using out-dated and discarded neckties, and restyling them into wearable clothing and pillows. Once your friends know what you're up too, you'll have more ties than you can imagine. The variations can be endless.

Combining neckties is like solving a jigsaw puzzle. Group them in color themes and let the tie shapes dictate the overall layout. Wool, silk, and cotton — any fiber will work. Save the labels, too. They add interest as surface embellishments.

Strip the neckties of their internal materials, removing labels, linings, interfacings, and stitching. Clean the ties to remove any stains or plan to cover a hard-to-remove blemish with a label. Press seam allowances flat.

Good-quality ties are cut on the bias, so stripes generally become diagonal stripes. Mix and match stripes, geometric designs, and allover patterns. Make one large square and fold the corners to the center to create a seamless pillow with a back opening.

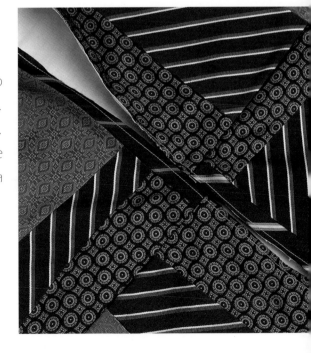

Chapter 2

A rectangle and two circles are the components for a bolster-style pillow. Seam the irregular edges of the neckties together. To stabilize the bias pieces, baste whole sections to a batiste or muslin backing before finishing the pillow.

Chapter 3

Ribbons are like candy — you can't have just one piece! Some people collect ribbons like others collect stamps or tools. I didn't know that collecting ribbons had any appeal until I found good ribbons and better yet, old ribbons. Buy them when you see them, and not necessarily when you need them. It feels okay to let them lie in a box, or on a shelf, or in a basket just as they are. But eventually, it feels even better to bring them out into the open, touch them, and let them speak to you — begging to be dressed and turned out for the ball.

CHRYSANTHEMUM PILLOW

This is a pillow that I like to call a chrysanthemum pillow. It resembles the flower with its multi-layered lettuce edges and button center. Use buttery, washed silk charmeuse or wash crepe de chine in the washing machine to get a soft, matte silk.

You will need a total of 1 3/4 yards of fabric. Cut nine strips of fabric from selvage to selvage, each 5" wide. Reserve the remaining fabric for the pillow back.

Using matching 100% silk thread, serge one long edge of each strip using a 3-thread rolled hem.

Send the nine strips of fabric to a professional pleating company (see the Resource List for more information) with instructions to mushroom pleat in a three to one ratio. The strips will be returned between paper and permanently pleated. Remove the paper from the fabric.

Sew the strips together, end to end, with a small French seam in the following order: Sew three strips together to form the first piece; sew two and one-half strips together to form a second piece; sew two strips together to form a third piece; and sew one and one-half strips together to form the last piece.

Finish the raw edges of the continuous strip pieces with a 4-thread overlock stitch, keeping the pleats intact as much as possible. Pull the right needle thread to gently gather the pieces and force them into a slight curve.

Draw a 15" circle on the basic fabric (this is the finished pillow size) and add 1/2" for seam allowances. Cut out the circle for the pillow top. Draw four circles, placing the first circle 3" inside the outer edge of the finished pillow line. Space the remaining three lines inside the first, 1 1/4" apart. Pin the first and longest piece along the first line. Straight-stitch along the line of serger stitches. Repeat pinning and stitching the next three rows using the longest to shortest pieces. Add a large decorative button in the center over the exposed serged edges on the inner and smallest circle.

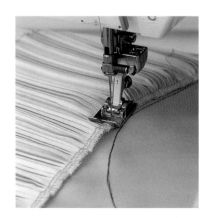

PLEATED RIBBON TRIMS

This is a sweet little stack of two pillows made from vintage metal fabrics. Metal cloth is a decorative fabric woven with silk or cotton lengthwise yarns, and gold, silver, aluminum or copper filler yarns. The fabric is considered precious and expensive, and it tarnishes. Ribbons play an important part in making these pillows — the pleated edge, the wrapping, and the flower.

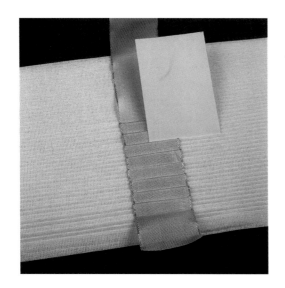

A special ribbon pleater, designed by ribbon artist Candace Kling, and produced and distributed by Lacis in Berkeley, makes pleating ribbon easy. Place the ribbon on top of the pleater and push it into the slots at regular intervals. You can skip any number of slots to vary the width of the pleats. A small piece of oak tag helps push the fabric evenly into the slots.

With a warm iron (test first!), press the pleats while still in the pleater. You may want to use a press cloth.

Remove the pleats from the pleater and stitch along one edge to secure them in place.

RIBBON EMBROIDERY

Classic embroidery stitches are enhanced when using hand-dyed, bias-cut, silk ribbon strands. Design inspirations are everywhere, especially in books, natural floral bouquets, and photographs.

Use silk ribbon, 3/8" to 1/2" wide, or make your own from bias-cut silk charmeuse and thread into a tapestry needle. A basic embroidery book is all you will need to re-create these stitches. The petals in the primary flower are formed by stitching long stitches in a pinecone shape, working from the center out and top down. Keep the bottom petals loose. Add three or four strands of embroidery floss, backstitching to form a stem and other floral accents.

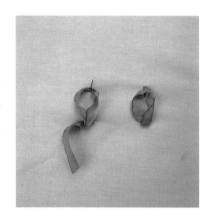

Another flower component utilizes a lazy daisy stitch. Form this stitch by bringing the needle up through the fabric. Loop the ribbon from left to right and pull the needle back through the fabric to the left of the first entry. Bring the needle up and over the top of the loop. Secure the top of the loop with one stitch.

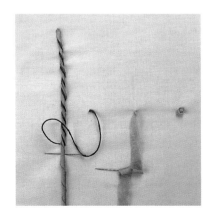

Stems and French knots are the little extras that add character. To form the stem, use silk ribbon or a silk charmeuse strip 1/2" wide. Thread a needle with either, then pull the ribbon up through the fabric, twist tightly, and pin down as you couch around it with embroidery floss. French knots use 1/4"-wide ribbon. Pull the ribbon flat towards you. Lay the needle on the ribbon and wrap the ribbon around the needle twice. Insert the needle into the fabric a few threads away from the original insertion point making the French knot.

HORSEHAIR BRAID

I discovered a fascinating combination of materials when shopping in a Chicago boutique a few years ago — a sheer jacket made with horsehair braid sewn to tulle or netting. The artist's design inspiration was wrought iron gates. I adapted the concept into a pillow surface and underlined it with a beautiful silk taffeta.

Horsehair braid is available in lots of colors as narrow as 1/2" and as wide as 6". There are usually matching or coordinating tulles. You'll need to experiment a bit, but I suggest selecting a narrow horsehair braid applied to a fairly coarse tulle.

Draw a design on paper first. Soft curves are easier to manipulate than small circles or sharp angles. Go over the design with a dark, medium-point magic marker. Place the tulle on top of the paper and trace the design using Clo-Chalk.

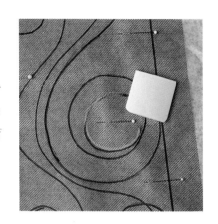

Using an open embroidery foot and changing the needle position, stitch along one edge of the horsehair braid over the marked design. Choosing to sew on the right or left edge of the braid changes the final effect and creates both convex and concave curves.

Wider horsehair braid can be used as the flange. The braid gets thick and thin as it is pulled, and it molds easily around a curve or corner.

Chapter 3

MITERED RIBBON FLANGE

A gutsy, tapestry ribbon adds texture and richness to a perfectly pleated silk pillow.
The ribbon is double-layered and makes easy work when making a flange.

Draw lines on the face of the fabric every 3". To form a 1 1/2" pleat, place the top edge of a 1 1/2"-wide oak tag template (see Chapter 1, Pillow Closures) along the marked line. Fold along the next marked line and bring the fold to the top of the template and press.

On the wrong side of the pressed pleats, using an edgestitch foot, move the needle position to the left and stitch along the edge of each pleat. This ensures that the pleats will stay in position. Baste along the finished pillow seam line.

To form the mitered corner, fold each end of the ribbon diagonally, matching centers, and press.

With a chalk marker, highlight the crease line that was formed. Stitch along the line and trim to 1/4". Press this seam open and trim the corner. Repeat on all four corners of both the top and bottom layers of the flange.

To complete the pillow, with wrong sides together, sew the front to the back, leaving an opening to insert the pillow form in the back. With wrong sides together, sew the two ribbon flanges around the outer edges only. Pin the front and back pillow sections between the two inner edges of the ribbon flange and sew through all four layers.

RIBBON WEAVING

Ribbon weaving is not a particularly new topic, but there has been a resurgence of interest in this old Victorian art form. Whereas traditional ribbon weaving tends to use the same ribbon type in an array of colors in definite patterns, it is always fun to experiment and take an art form to a different place by changing widths, mixing colors and textures, and adding a surprise element.

Hand-dyed, bias-cut silk charmeuse in two widths, sheer metallic, and narrow, delicate silk ribbons are combined in a repeating pattern to weave a ribbon pillow front. Coordinating cable cord and matching tassels outline the pillow.

Chapter 3

RIBBON WORK

72

Some of the most beautiful velvet ribbons are vintage. The colors tend to be richer and maybe a little bit odd. Sometimes they are aged and mottled, only to make them more interesting. And they appear in the strangest places. A sheer ribbon overlay on this pillow distorts some of the fading where the bolt of ribbon had been on a shelf for too many years.

Weaving requires a pinning surface such as a blocking board. To make a blocking board, place cotton or polyester batting over a piece of unfinished plywood. Wrap a piece of heavy duck canvas or a gridded ironing board cover around the edges. Staple on the bottom side.

Place a piece of stable, woven, fusible interfacing, such as So Sheer™, on the blocking board with the glue side up. Make sure the interfacing is larger than the finished ribbon weaving. Draw the pillow outline on the interfacing. Lay the ribbons face up, vertically and parallel to one another. Secure the ends of the ribbons with good, glass head pins. Attach a bodkin to the end of a ribbon strip and weave horizontally. Continue weaving parallel ribbons until the pillow surface is complete.

To determine the amount of ribbon needed, make a practice section of one repeat and multiply by the number of repeats.

After the ribbons have been woven, adjust them until you are satisfied that they are even. Pin again where necessary. Place a press cloth over the work and fuse the ribbons to the interfacing backing.

When fusing velvet ribbons, use terry cloth as a press cloth so as not to flatten the velvet pile.

Mark the finished pillow size and sew along the marking as a reference line for assembling the pillow.

LAPPED RIBBON

The inspiration for this pillow was the 1995 edition of a summer Ferragamo hand-bag. Wide grosgrain ribbons were sewn to another faille-type fabric in horizontal bands and topped off with a bamboo handle. Simple and elegant!

So instead of real bamboo, I used it as the color in my ribbon selection. It's not grosgrain, but vintage, variegated silk ribbon, and it's sewn to a damask ground along one edge. Each ribbon layer ever so slightly overlaps the next ribbon.

The purity of white, of linen — simplicity is such a relief. Sometimes, it's more difficult to pare down than to add to. But the combination of white and other neutrals with pure linen, silk, and cotton can only be interpreted into chic, sleek, and cool. The word tailored doesn't mean plain. It's more about well-finished, simple lines. Organza over linen, cut velvet, satin, silk taffeta, sheer, and lots and lots of linen are both current and timeless.

Chapter 4

TAILORED PILLOWS

EDGES AND CORNERS — IDEAS AND TECHNIQUES

Fine-linen stores specializing in European bedding and other specialty linens are wonderful sources of inspiration for great edge details.

Hemstitching is a term referring to the removal of some of the weft and warp threads, then grouping the remaining threads using different stitches to create a line or border. Traditionally, this type of drawn thread work has been done by hand. But a machine version is attainable. Select a triple zigzag stitch with a 2mm width and 1 1/2mm stitch length. Using a wing needle (size #100 - #120), stitch forward the desired length. Leave the needle in the fabric, raise the presser foot, and pivot the work 360° so that you are stitching back along the previous row of stitching. The wing needle penetrates the same center hole several times and creates a pattern in the weave.

For the best hemstitching results, spray a heavy application of fabric stiffener or spray starch on the fabric and press. Also, use 2-ply cotton embroidery thread.

Many of the newer-model sewing machines have a large scallop stitch and even some of the older models have the ability to elongate a smaller scallop. Sew a scallop stitch of any size on the fabric. A tear-away stabilizer placed under the fabric will keep the work flat. Using small, very sharp, craft scissors, trim the excess fabric next to the line of stitching.

The mark of a good sewing machine is the quality of the satin stitch. Using rayon decorative thread in the needle and bobbin, stitch a zigzag stitch set at a 3mm width and satin-stitch length. Stop at the corner and tie off on the wrong side. Overlap the stitching and start again for another side.

Threading a #3.0/90 double needle and sewing a straight line about 2" from the edge creates another version of a linen detail. Fill in the corner with a 3mm-wide zigzag stitch.

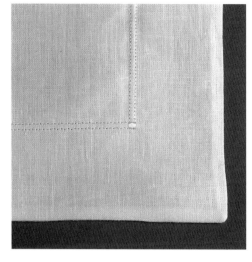

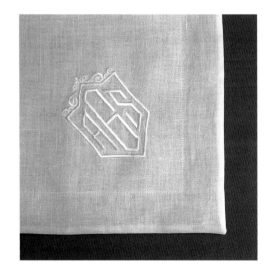

With the introduction of embroidery machines into the home sewing market, we now have the ability to emulate great embroidery designs such as the monogram shown here. Decorative rayon thread adds brilliance to the design.

A fine gimp braid used in the interior decorating industry adds just a hint of a scallop to an edge. Center the braid on the wrong side of the linen, along the edge, and edgestitch to secure. To turn a corner, clip between the scallops.

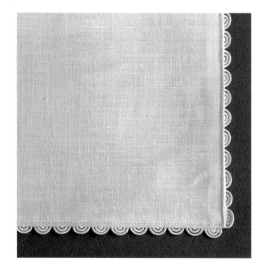

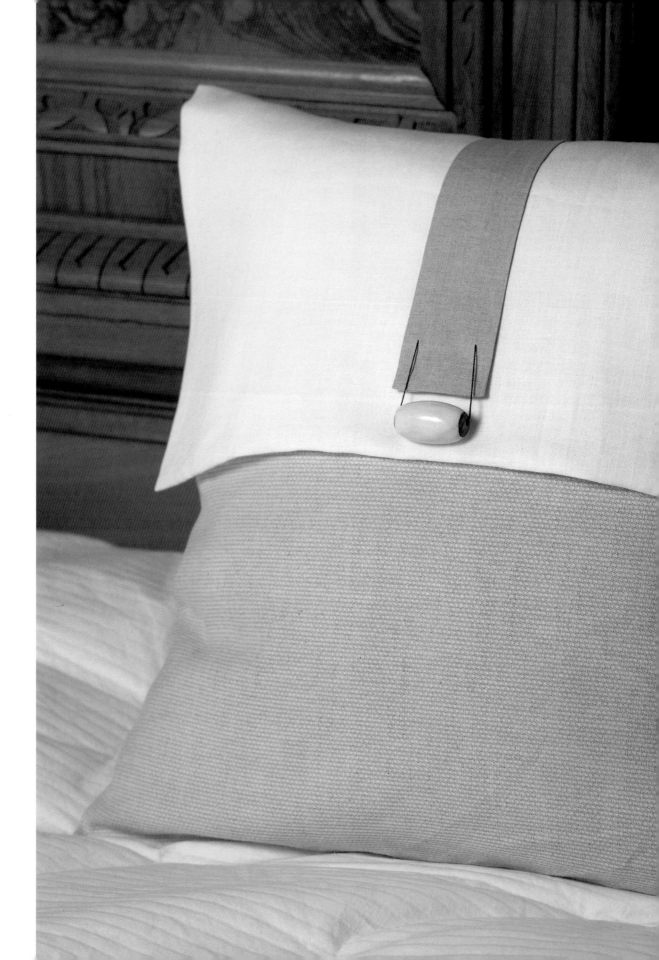

TAILORED

ENVELOPE FOLD

Sometimes the opening for stuffing the pillow can be integrated into the overall design. Nothing more than a plain paper envelope was the inspiration for this pillow.

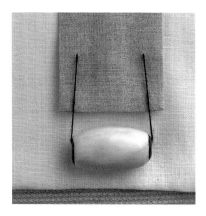

The white linen envelope flap is held in place by a fabric tab weighted by a threaded ceramic bead.

TAILORED

WRAPPED BUNDLE

A simple pillow wrap becomes extraordinary when the fabric is spectacular. I placed a layer of silk batting under the silk cut-velvet to intensify the softness even more.

The combination of a jade ring tied with satiny rattail and embellished with a sterling-silver-and-amethyst handmade button makes a truly exquisite closure.

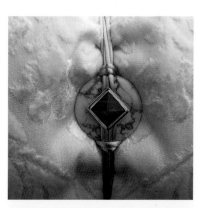

MITERED TAFFETA ON SHEER

White-on-white reminds me of a Newport Beach verandah in the summer. The white sheer burnt-out fabric is bordered with white silk taffeta. The mitered corner is the trick. A silk taffeta pillow is inserted into this pillow casing.

Learning this mitered banding technique opened my eyes to the possibilities of totally finished edges on both garments and home furnishings. It took years of sewing before I even knew about this technique. Now it's one of the staples in my sewing repertoire.

To form an outward mitered corner, begin by cutting a strip of fabric four times the finished width of the band. Press the strip in half lengthwise. Then press each raw edge to the center crease line.

TAILORED

With right sides together, align the raw edges of the band and the pillow edge and stitch along the first crease line. End the stitching at a point from the corner which equals the finished width of the band. Backstitch to secure.

At the ending point of the stitching, fold the band diagonally, away from the pillow. Then, fold the band straight down, matching the fold to the two raw edges and aligning the other raw edges.

Keeping the opposite raw edge folded to the center crease, draw an arrow from the ending point of the stitching diagonally to the folded edge at the center crease and back down to the opposite edge, parallel with the starting point. Stitch along the marked line through the band only. Continue stitching the band to the pillow along the first crease line.

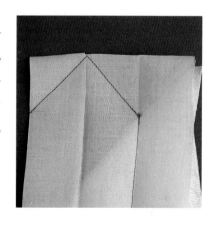

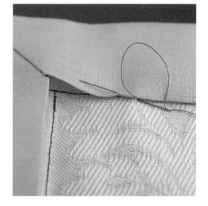

Turn the band to the back and slip-stitch the folded edge to the seam allowance stitching line. Some amount of trimming may need to be done, depending on the bulk of the fabric.

PIPED AND DOUBLE-RUFFLED

Light, layered, and lengthened — this pillow is almost like a sampler of techniques. An unusual cotton fabric resembling a clipped spot technique is just sheer enough to require underlining with silk douppioni. The panels are separated by a wonderful piping method that I learned from Laura Hotchkiss Brown, a teacher at The Sewing Workshop. The outer ruffle, edged with a baby hem, veils the crushed ruffles.

This piping technique makes a beautiful finished connection between an opaque fabric and a sheer fabric. Cut a piece of bias fabric twice the width of the finished piping plus two seam allowances. Working on the opaque fabric, with right sides together and matching raw edges, stitch down the center of the bias strip.

TAILORED

Fold the bias in half, pressing against the stitching and matching all of the raw edges. Stitch through all layers. The distance from the fold is the width of the finished piping. Use a special presser foot called a 1/4" or quilting foot which is designed to create a perfect 1/4" seam from the center needle position to the edge of the foot.

With right sides together, place the opaque layer over the sheer layer. Stitch along the previous stitching line closest to the raw edge.

Separate the sheer and opaque panels. Turn all seam allowances toward the opaque panel and stitch in the ditch on the right side. Trim, if necessary.

Create a fine baby hem on the edge of the top ruffle. Fold the edge of the fabric to the wrong side along the finished hemline. Stitch as close to the fold as possible. An edgestitch foot, with the needle position to the left, is extremely useful in being able to sew straight and close.

Trim the excess fabric close to the stitching. I have discovered two pieces of equipment that make this easy work. Appliqué scissors allow you to get really close to the stitching without fear of cutting the outer fabric by mistake. A third "hand", which attached to both your fabric and to a stationary object, keeps the work taut so that the trimming is much easier and even.

Fold the fabric again and stitch on top of the first stitching line. With practice, you will increase your ability to get this hem very small, no more than 1/8" wide.

To make the second ruffle, a crushed ruffle, cut a piece of fabric twice the finished width plus two seam allowances, and twice the finished length. With right sides together, fold the fabric in half lengthwise and stitch the ends. To get a crisp pressed edge, press the seam allowance open first over a wood point presser before turning.

An easy way to gather fabric is to insert cotton gimp cord through a small hole in the front of the presser foot and zigzag over the cord. Secure the gimp cord at one end and pull the other end of the cord, adjusting the gathers evenly and to the correct length. Secure the other end of the gimp cord by wrapping it around a pin. Insert the seam allowance of the ruffle into the seam to finish.

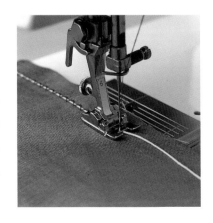

TAILORED

TASSELED CIRCLE

Appliqué and reverse appliqué techniques have one pitfall. There is always a raw edge that needs to be dealt with, either by stitching over the edge in some fashion or turning it under. This pillow demonstrates a clean way to create a refined edge on a circular shape.

Draw a large circle on a piece of oak tag. Most compasses are not large enough for the size of circle needed. This set of posts attaches to a 1"-wide ruler and is easily adjusted for any size circle. Cut out the template.

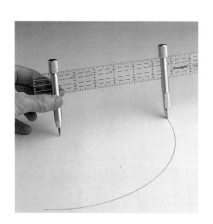

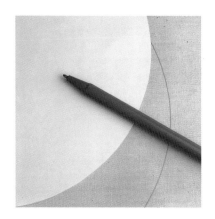

Using the template, trace the circle shape onto the outer fabric, using an air-soluble marking pen. Using a small stitch length, stitch along the marked line.

Cut out the center of the circle, leaving a 1/4" seam allowance. With sharp trimming scissors, clip at regular intervals to the stitching line.

TAILORED

Using the remaining section of the oak tag, press the seam allowance back and over the template to the wrong side.

With wrong side to right side, position the circle opening over the under layer of fabric and edgestitch in place. Cable cord trim can be couched to the circular edge with matching thread. Use a cording foot that has a special cutout on the underside to accommodate the cord.

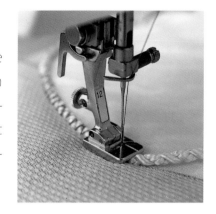

The central embellishment consists of a decorative tassel and a large vintage button, both attached with a small silk covered button.

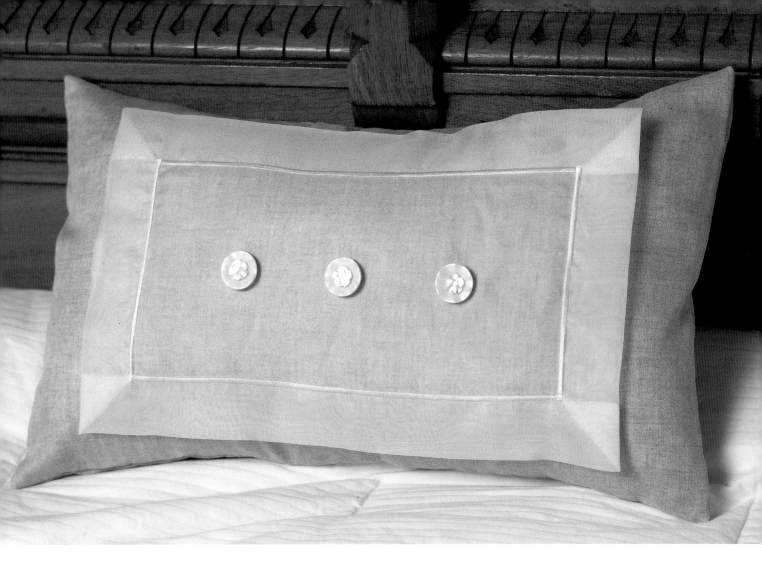

ORGANZA SQUARE ON LINEN

A silk organza pinafore garnishes a pure linen pillow. It's a simple application — edges folded back about 1 1/2", satin stitching concealing the raw edges and sewn to the linen at the same time.

For the three-button embellishment, two pearl buttons and one miniature floret on a larger fluted edge are stacked to add dimension and resemble a flower.

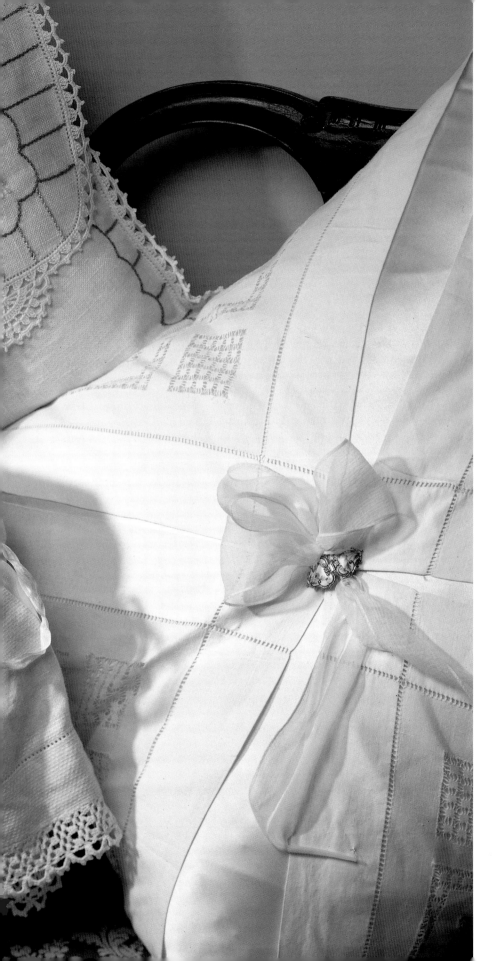

HEIRLOOM PILLOWS

Chapter 5

Our attics and
closets are full
of beautiful linens
and laces sewn
by important
women in
our lives whom
we have never
met. It's
time to take these
heirlooms out
of the closet and
let them see the
light of day.
Tablecloths, towels,
pillowcases,
and other lost
pieces of our past
can be recycled
and restyled
into useful
additions to our
homes or
become great
works of art.

VINTAGE LINENS — PRESERVING AND LAUNDERING

There are many theories concerning the care and laundering of old linens. My assessment of the information that is available on the subject is that all probably work, so it is necessary to find the right combination of procedures and products for your individual projects. Here's an overview from some good sources:

Kaethe Kliot, of Lacis in Berkeley, California, is a leading expert in the conservation and restoration of fine lace and textiles. To extract imbedded stains and soil on fine lace, she recommends an hour-long presoak in an enzyme-protein solution such as Biz™ or Axion™ and then soak for as long as it takes for the stain to come out. Rinse until the wash water runs clear. Lay small pieces of lace on glass to dry or place larger pieces flat on a sheet. Store large pieces, folded in boxes, lined and layered with acid-free paper. Store small pieces on cardboard such as paper towel tubes. Never use plastic for storage.

Amy Endries, owner of Hotzy Totzy, a business specializing in artful reconstruction, sends the most delicate fabrics to a good dry cleaner and handwashes anything else in Ivory™ liquid dish soap.

Tricia Foley, author of <u>Linens and Lace</u>, also handwashes, without rubbing or agitation, in Ivory™ or Orvus™. Mix four tablespoons of Ivory™ or one tablespoon of Orvus™ with a gallon of warm water. Line the sink with a towel to use as a sling to lift the wet textile. Soak for 45 minutes and rinse for 45 minutes. Keeping the piece in the wet sling, place it into a dry towel and blot, changing towels as often as necessary until the piece is more damp than wet. Lay it on a Formica™, glass, or non-wooden surface, and reshape. Press linens while they are still damp. In addition to storing in acid-free paper, a cardboard, metal, or wooden box lined with unbleached muslin also works.

Many fine linen stores recommend a washing product called Linen Wash® by LeBlanc. I have used it and like it so well that I use it for almost all of my laundry.

To remove a stubborn stain or freshen a discolored piece, try soaking it in a mixture of fresh-squeezed lemon juice and water and then hanging it outdoors in the sun. In all of the information about spot removing, using bleach is never recommended.

The bleaching fields of Flanders were famous for their magical, still-dewy lawns for drying. The combination of dew, grass, and sun were so powerful, that linens from all over Europe were sent there to be cared for.

Even with all this expert advice, sometimes old linens are too tired to respond to good cleaning methods. Tinting or dyeing are two ways to rehabilitate an old textile. Tinting is as simple as using tea, such as Celestial Seasonings Cranberry Cove, for a pale blush color, instant tea for ecru, or coffee for a darker tone. Rit™ dye is just fine for getting more intense color changes.

HEIRLOOM

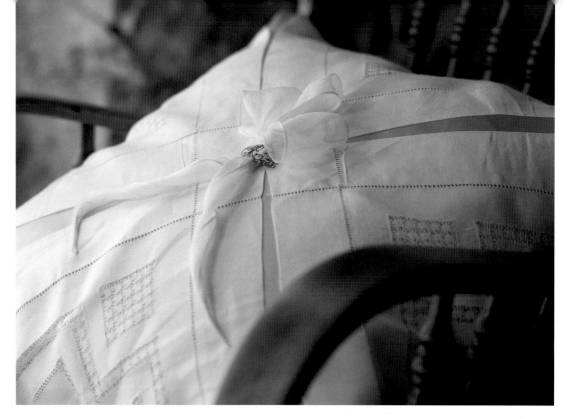

SQUARE TABLECLOTH

Four corners of a square linen tablecloth with drawnwork embellishment are stitched together to encase a silk charmeuse pillow.

A soft, sheer silk ribbon bow is secured with an antique cloisonné clasp adorning the center of the tablecloth pillow.

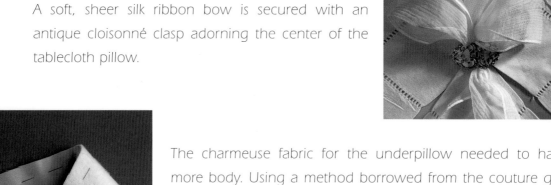

The charmeuse fabric for the underpillow needed to have more body. Using a method borrowed from the couture garment industry when underlining dress bodices and silk jackets, the silk charmeuse is underlined with a double-faced diaper flannel. Baste the outer fabric and flannel together around the edges and treat the piece as one layer in the construction of the pillow.

TOWEL BOLSTERS

Antique hand towels are usually the right shape to re-style into a bolster pillow. The sail boat design and border on one towel is hand-appliquéd, Crocheted lace was added to the edge of another towel on the second bolster.

To close the pillow, overlap the long edges and add button-holes and heirloom pearl buttons to the hem allowances. To create a casing, sew a strip of rayon seam binding to the wrong side. Feed a twisted tie or ribbon through a buttonhole and draw up to close the ends of the pillow.

Another way to close the ends is to use seam binding as the "thread" and hand-sew long gathering stitches along the edges.

HEIRLOOM

ENVELOPE TABLE RUNNER

An embroidered table runner with crocheted lace edges and scalloped ends is easily transformed into an envelope pillow. The hardest part in making this pillow was cutting off one scalloped end! The easy part was hemming that end, folding the runner, wrong sides together, and stitching up the sides.

LAYERED LACES

Reflections of the Victorian era are the influence for many of our interiors today. Entire magazines and books are dedicated to the Victorian arts and lifestyle. Bringing a wonderful collage of the era's finest into one, this pillow consists of layered, scrunched, stuffed, and fluffed laces and fabric yardage.

Sources for the interesting lace and fabrics are everywhere. Crocheted doilies, lampshade trims, hat decorations, old garments, embroidered fragments to cut apart, and, of course, perfectly intact and preserved linens are found in flea markets, antique shops, estate sales, or garage sales. Small shops specializing in vintage linens are emerging, too.

This pillow begins with a backing fabric of a medium-pink-colored poly-satin pinned to a piece of foam core with a fairly large piece of lace yardage placed on top of the poly-satin. Bits and pieces of lace and ribbons are arranged on the fabric in a pleasing manner. Once the design is finalized, the fabric is removed from the foam core surface and a curved upholstery needle threaded with one strand of quilting thread holds it all together. Rayon seam binding, lampshade gimp, silk flowers, and other trims are applied last.

HEIRLOOM

DREAM PILLOW

I made my first dream pillow under the tutelage of Lynda Albiero, a Northern California artist specializing in sachets and small sewn accessories, and a teacher at The Sewing Workshop. Of course, her dream pillows are mostly about the incredible potpourri that fills an inner pillow and encourages pleasant dreams. My version is enlarged, has nothing to do with scent, but has a lot to do with beautiful fabrics and trim combinations and is used as an accent pillow. The pillow-case is silk peau de soie satin and the inner pillow is crin-kled silk sheer.

The 9" x 15" inner pillow is one long rectangle folded twice and overlapped in the center. The baby hem at the opening edges requires a little glue stick adhesive to get the sewing started. Self-filled bias tubes tie the pillow together. It can be filled with potpourri, scented leaves, or silk batting.

Chapter 5

HEIRLOOM

Vintage lace tops the gathered crinkled silk ruffle. A double-layered ribbon trim adorned with crystal leaves connects the pillow and ruffle.

Since the outer pillowcase is open at one end, the seam is finished on the inside with a French seam. With wrong sides together, sew a narrow 1/4" seam. Using a straight edge and a rotary cutter, trim the seam to a scant 1/8".

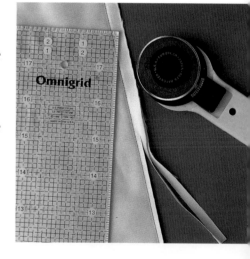

For a crisp edge, press the seam allowance open over a wood point presser.

102

With right sides together, turn the fabrics and sew a scant 1/4" seam, encasing the raw edges. Look for little whiskers coming through the seam and trim.

Some fabrics are tricky to gather, especially wiry sheers and silks. A gathering foot on a serger can really control these types of fabrics. Upon completion and if more gathering is needed, gently pull the right needle thread to gather a little more.

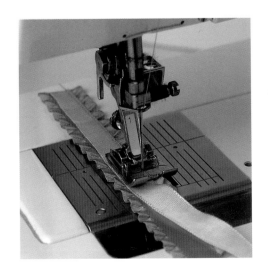

A ruffled silk ribbon was not quite the right shade, so a narrower grosgrain ribbon was sewn down the center of the silk ribbon, exposing only the ruffled edges and altering the overall look.

Chapter 6

Shape and design — the geometry of pillows. To play with pillow shapes is like working with a puzzle. Sometimes a ruler and a little math works just fine; sometimes there are objects that can simply be copied. Sorting it all out is the fun. By the way, who decided that a pillow could only be a square, a rectangle, or a circle? Odd-shaped pillows that are more than just interesting on the surface are real statements, like art. Use them one at a time as a focal point, or group and mix them for high impact.

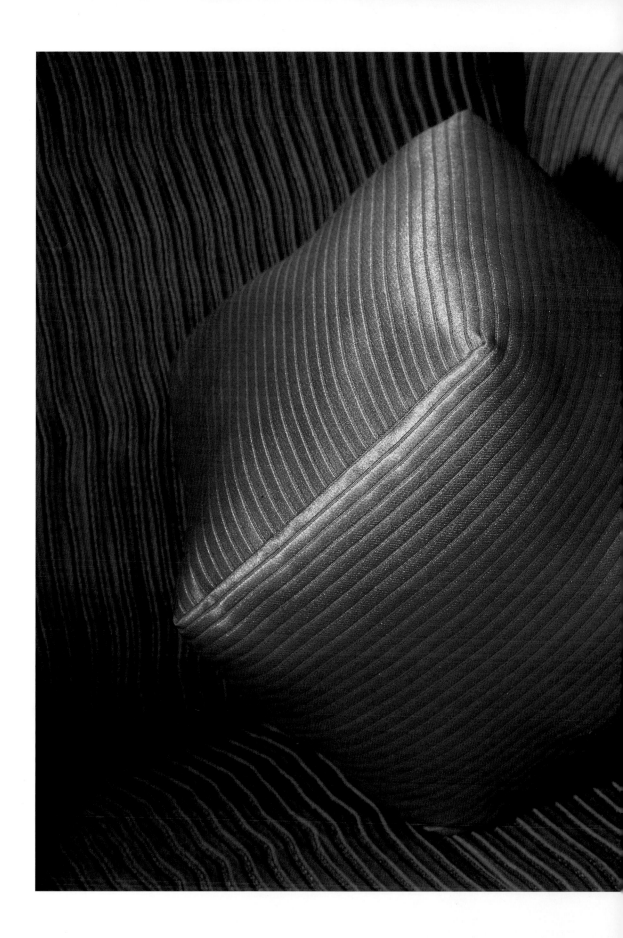

UNIQUE SHAPES

Chapter 6

THE CUBE

I've been told that a person's doodling in the margins of their paperwork is a real personality indicator. My doodles are squares and boxes. It's my favorite shape. Naturally, I think a cube pillow is perfectly acceptable.

The cube pillow can be constructed from a single T-shaped piece. See the pattern (page 114) included for you, which is easier to sew than fitting and sewing six separate pieces. The look is cleaner, too. This is one time that I recommend a zipper closure. It helps retain the firm shape.

The fabric used in this pillow is a lustrous silk ottoman which has a subtle tone-on-tone pattern. Ottoman is a plain-weave fabric with large, round horizontal cords. Patterned fabrics of all kinds lend themselves to cube pillows.

There are two kinds of corners to sew on this pillow, inside and outside. Reinforce the outside corners with small stitches and clip to the corner point. Fold the pillow, matching the raw edges. Beginning at the inside corners, make sure to start stitching at precisely the point. Stitch in one continuous line to the zipper opening. At the outside corner, sew just inside the reinforcement stitches, pivoting at the clipped point. Repeat for the other side.

UNIQUE SHAPES

THE FREE FORM & THE BALL

The mathematical formula for making the wedge shapes for a ball or sphere pillow is too difficult to comprehend. So the simplest thing to do is trace the shape from a basketball which already has the lines on it. Or use the pattern (page 115) included in this chapter to cut the necessary eight sections.

For a smoother shape, cut the wedges on the bias. In some cases, you may want to play with the pattern in the fabric. So, it is acceptable to cut them however you choose.

With right sides together, place two wedge pieces together and stitch from top to bottom. It is important to stop and start exactly at the top and bottom points. Continue adding wedge shapes, leaving a 4" opening in the last seam. Sew 1/4" seams to prevent the need for trimming and allowing the seams to lie flat.

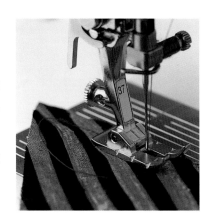

Lois Ericson, textile artist and author, has written about a method of weaving fabrics using shaped strips. This technique inspired this free-form pillow made from black-and-silver duoppioni silk.

To make the fabric used in the free-form pillow, begin with two like-size pieces of fabric. Out of one piece, cut some vertical random strips in soft, curvilinear shapes, and out of the other piece, cut similar but random horizontal shapes.

Pin a piece of lightweight fusible interfacing with the fusible side up to a blocking board or piece of foam core (see Chapter 3 - Ribbon Work Pillows). With the right sides up, lay the vertical strips in order of cutting and weave the horizontal pieces through them. Fuse the two layers to the backing.

Choose a contrasting or coordinating thread color and satin-stitch over the raw edges and through all layers. Cut a pillow shape, emulating one of the free-form shapes.

THE TRIANGLE

Marcy Tilton, the founder of The Sewing Workshop, has always loved cloth but recently has taken to paper. She's stamping it, painting it, folding it, and pretty soon, she will be making it. I didn't want a paper pillow for this book (although the idea has some merit), so she borrowed from the traditional art of Japanese paper folding, origami, and produced these pillows. The closures are as interesting as the basic shapes. The applied squares and trimmed edges are inspired from the construction of a traditional triangle box. A simplified version of the origami box is included as a pattern (page 116).

Turn under 1" seam allowances on all edges of the triangle pillow pattern and press. Fold the fabric, wrong sides together, and edgestitch along the center fold line first. Continue edgestitching the four additional triangular lines as marked.

Apply narrow ribbon or braid along one end of the rectangle, wrapping the ends to the wrong sides to finish. Edgestitch along the inner edge of the ribbon.

Fold under 1/2" seam allowances on all sides of the small square and press. Fold the square diagonally along the fold line and press. Sew decorative ribbon or braid along two edges, mitering the corner, as it is sewn.

Fold the rectangle along fold line "D", and matching points "C". Edgestitch from "D" to "C" on both sides.

Place the remaining edges together, matching "A" to "A" and "B" to "B". Edgestitch one-half of the seam together and stuff the pillow. Slip-stitch the remaining one-half of the seam together and place the small rectangle diagonally over the center of the seam, matching the edges of the square to the dotted placement lines.

THE SHOPPING BAG

My friend and long-time associate, Dort Johnson, has an unusual sense of humor. When I asked her to contribute to this book, she produced "the shopping bag." It is whimsical and outrageous, and women can relate to it. Make the "bag" from camel-colored faux suede and fill it with velvet fruit.

The pattern is simple. You probably have plenty of paper bags in your house that you could use. Take a brown paper bag of any size apart and you have the pattern, or use the pattern (pages 117-118) included in this book.

Edgestitching is used to define the standard fold lines of the bag. Complete all of the steps on the inside or wrong side of the fabric, first, before moving to the outside.

THE STAR

A pewter serving tray from my favorite accessory store, Home Collections in Topeka, Kansas, was the inspiration for the shape of the star pillow. I traced around it and added about 1 1/2" to all sides to increase its size. Use the pattern (page 119) included in this book, enlarge it on a copy machine, or draw it again in full scale for your own star.

I guess it was destiny for me to write a book about pillows. My love for sewing, fabrics, and interior design have all come together. This simple shape, a star, is my sign of good fortune.

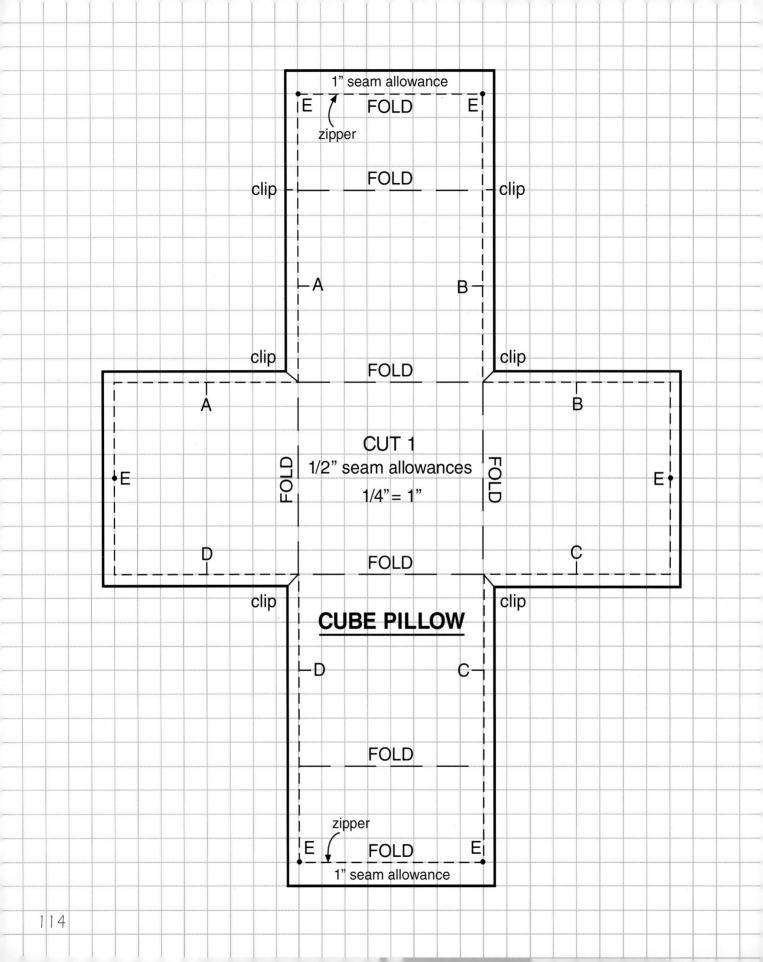

1" seam allowance

E   FOLD   E

↱ zipper

clip   FOLD   clip

A   B

clip   clip

A   B

E   CUT 1   E
1/2" seam allowances
1/4"= 1"

D   FOLD   C

clip   clip

CUBE PILLOW

D   C

FOLD

zipper
E ↓   FOLD   E
1" seam allowance

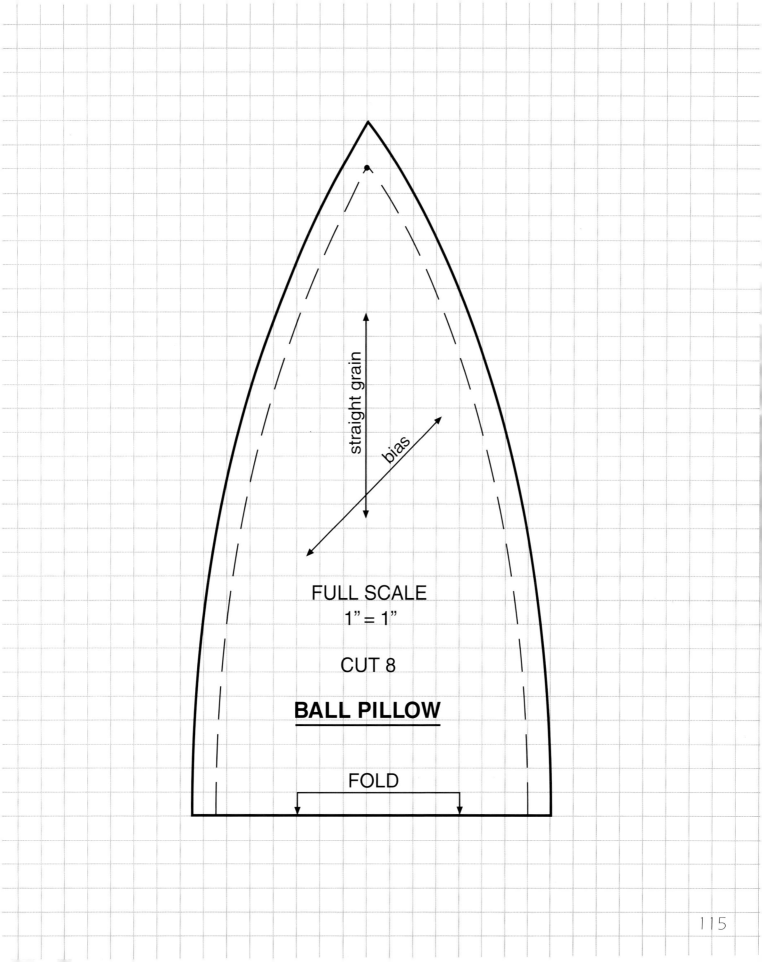

straight grain

bias

FULL SCALE
1" = 1"

CUT 8

BALL PILLOW

FOLD

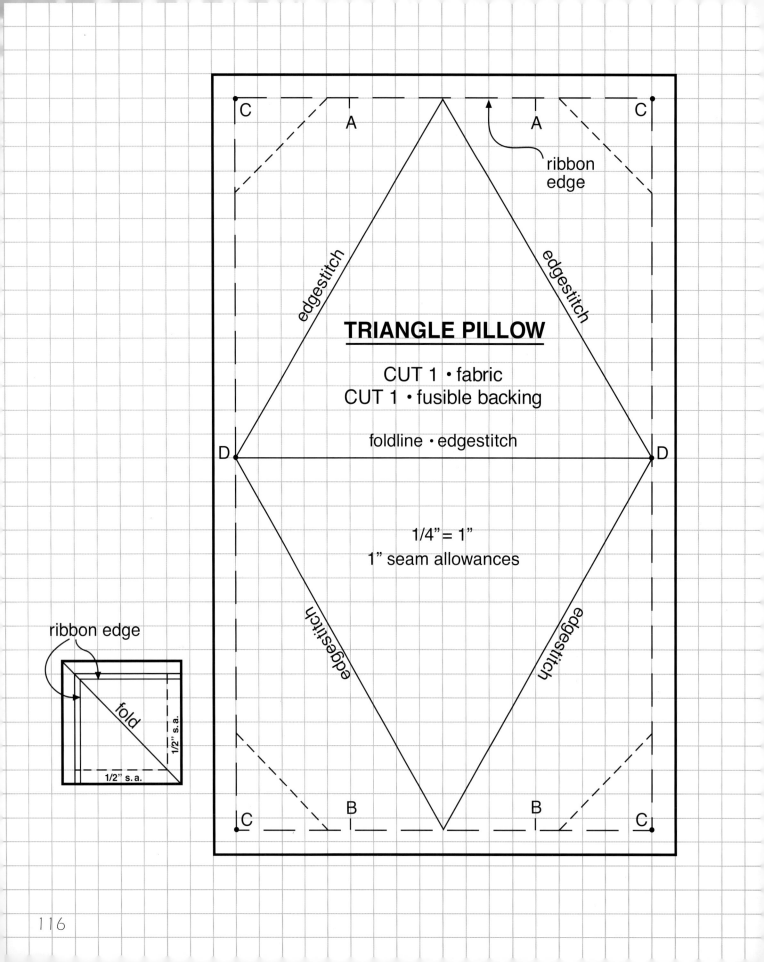

ribbon edge

C · · · A · · · A ↰ ribbon edge · · · C

edgestitch · · · edgestitch

TRIANGLE PILLOW

CUT 1 • fabric
CUT 1 • fusible backing

D · · · foldline • edgestitch · · · D

1/4" = 1"
1" seam allowances

edgestitch · · · edgestitch

ribbon edge

fold

1/2" s.a.

1/2" s.a.

C · · · B · · · B · · · C

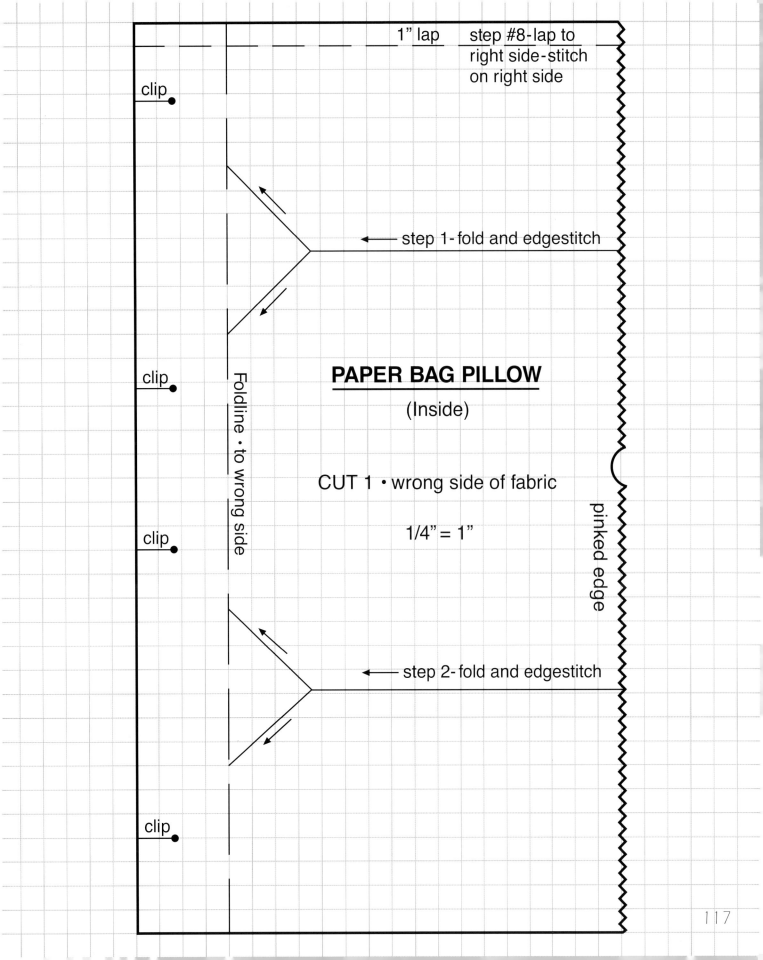

1" lap   step #8-lap to
right side-stitch
on right side

clip

step 1- fold and edgestitch

clip

Foldline · to wrong side

PAPER BAG PILLOW

(Inside)

clip

CUT 1 · wrong side of fabric

1/4" = 1"

pinked edge

clip

step 2- fold and edgestitch

clip

117

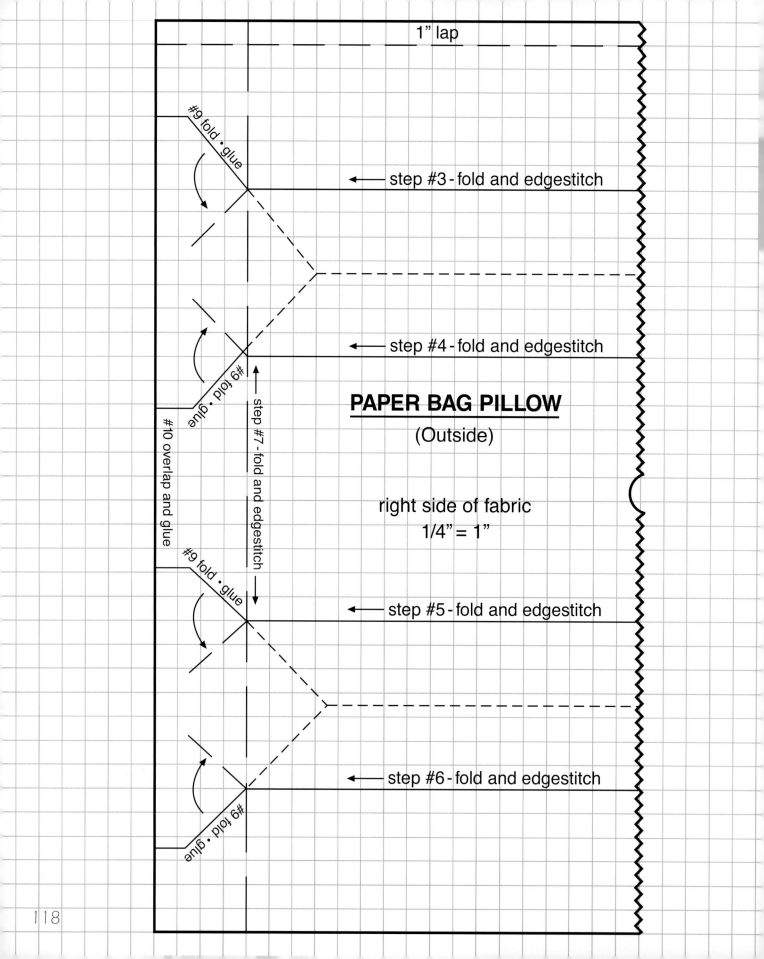

1" lap

#9 fold • glue

← step #3 - fold and edgestitch

#9 fold • glue

← step #4 - fold and edgestitch

#10 overlap and glue

step #7 - fold and edgestitch

PAPER BAG PILLOW

(Outside)

right side of fabric
1/4" = 1"

#9 fold • glue

← step #5 - fold and edgestitch

#9 fold • glue

← step #6 - fold and edgestitch

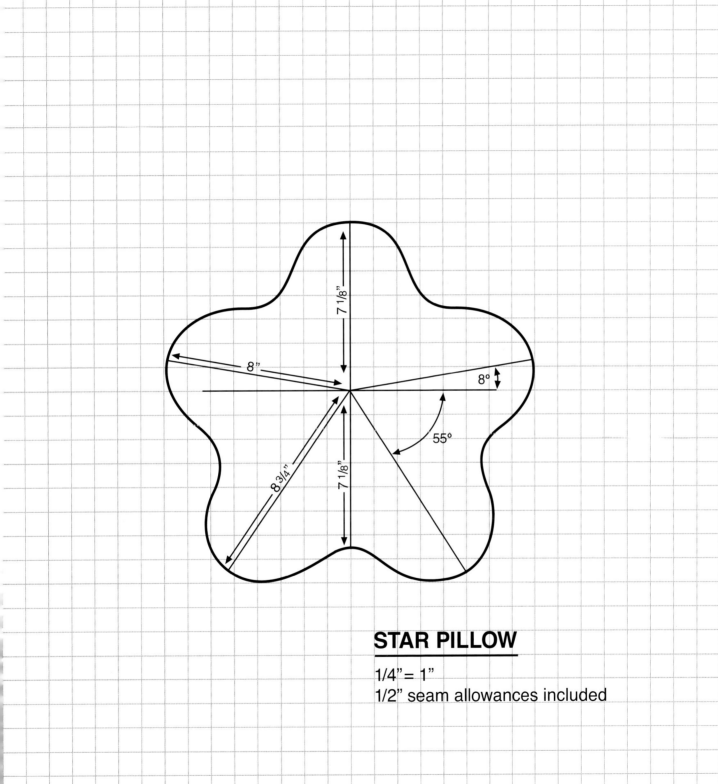

STAR PILLOW

1/4" = 1"
1/2" seam allowances included

Backstitch - Technique for stitching backward to secure the threads at the beginning and end of a seam.

Bias - Any cut which is not on the lengthwise grain or crossgrain. True bias is a line at a 45° angle to the lengthwise grain.

Blindstitch - An inconspicuous stitch for holding hems and facings in place.

Bodkin - Sharp, slender tool used to pull fabrics through narrow enclosed spaces, such as casings, or used to attach to one end of a ribbon when ribbon weaving.

Burn-out - Plain-weave fabric made of two different yarns. The fabric is treated with acid to "burn-out" one of the fibers, creating a pattern design. Most are lightweight blends with sheer and opaque areas; others are sculptured velvets.

Charmeuse - Soft, satin-weave fabric with a dull back and lustrous face. May be silk, polyester, cotton, rayon, or blends.

Chiffon - Lightweight, transparent, plain-weave fabric made with fine, highly twisted yarns. Soft, drapable, filmy and strong.

China Silk - Inexpensive, soft; lightweight silk made in a plain weave. Not very durable.

Cord - Plies of yarns that have been twisted together to form a single strand as filler.

Corded Piping - A bias strip of fabric with a cord inserted into the center.

Couching - Sewing a decorative cord, thread, or yarn to the surface of the fabric by stitching over the cord with the machine or by hand.

Crepe de Chine - Fine, light-to-medium-weight silk fabric with crepe yarns used in the warp and filling. Term means "silk from China."

Damask - Reversible fabric made on a jacquard loom. Features elaborate designs woven in cotton, linen, wool, worsted, silk, rayon, or manmade yarns. Usually has the same color warp and filling. Flatter than brocade.

Douppioni - Uneven, irregular yarn with slubs. Fabric was originally made of silk thread from two cocoons which had nested together. Both silk and synthetic fibers are used today.

Edgestitch - Topstitching 1/16" from an edge or seamline.

Faux Suede - A generic term for fabrics that have a suede-like appearance such as Ultrasuede™.

Flange - A projecting rim or extension to cord or corded piping.

French Seam - A self-finished seam that looks like a plain seam on the right side and a small, neat tuck on the wrong side. The raw edges are encased.

Gathers - Small, soft folds made by drawing fabric up on a line of hand or machine stitching.

Gimp - A flat braid-like trimming of silk, wool, or other cord.

Hemstitch - A decorative, open-weave stitching line produced by using a wing needle and a triple zigzag stitch or other decorative stitches.

Horsehair Braid - A stiff, bias braid woven of transparent synthetic yarns used to stiffen hem edges or embellish surfaces.

Miter - To join two edges at an angle, frequently at 45°.

Oak Tag - A manila-colored, lightweight cardboard used to make pressing and stitching templates.

Organza - Transparent, lightweight, plain-weave cloth with a stiff finish. Similar to cotton organdy, but made in silk, rayon, or polyester. Not as crisp as organdy.

Pattern Repeat - The vertical distance required for one complete design on the fabric pattern.

Peau de Soie - French term meaning "skin of silk." Medium-weight, satin-weave fabric with a dull finish. May be of silk, polyester, or other manmade fibers.

Piping - A flat, narrow fabric or braid used to finish raw edges on material.

Rattail - A small, shiney, tubular cord used as decorative cording or as a filler.

Reverse Appliqué - A method of creating dimensional textures by overlapping pieces of fabric, stitching them together, and trimming layers away to expose secondary fabrics.

Roll Hem - A method of turning the fabric to conceal a raw edge. May be done by hand, or on a sewing machine or serger.

Satin Stitch - Zigzag stitch of any width in a very short stitch.

Seams Great™ - A narrow, transparent bias webbing used to wrap the raw edges of a fabric to prevent raveling.

Shirring - Formed by numerous rows of gathers and is both decorative and functional.

Ottoman - Cross-rib fabric. Ribs can be small, medium, or large. Fabric weight varies with rib size.

Slipstitch - An almost invisible hand stitch done by sliding the needle through a folded edge and at the same point picking up a thread of the under fabric.

So Sheer™ - A lightweight, woven interfacing with a fusible backing used to stiffen and reinforce fabrics.

Spinster - A hand-held turning and spinning device that twists multiple strands of yarn to form decorative cord.

Staystitch - To straightstitch a single layer of fabric just inside the seamline.

Taffeta - Smooth, crisp, plain-weave fabric made of silk, acetate, rayon, nylon, polyester, or blends. Rustles when moved and holds its shape when draped.

Tapestry - Decorative fabric with woven designs which may be floral or tell a story.

Template - A tag board shape used to aid in pressing and stitching.

Topstitch - To stitch on the right side of the fabric in a designated width.

Tubing - Woven or knitted fabric in a cylindrical form.

Tulle - Very fine knit resembling netting. May be cotton, silk, or nylon.

Turkish Corner - A soft, decorative corner formed by folding and pressing the points at a corner before stitching.

Underlining - Fabric layer applied to the wrong side of the fabric before the seams are sewn.

Velvet - Luxurious fabric with a short (less than 1/8") pile on a knit or woven background. Made with an extra set of warp yarns. May be silk, rayon, nylon, or cotton. Ranges from lightweight transparent velvet to heavy upholstery velvet.

Welting - A fabric-covered cord sewn on a seam or used as a border.

BIBLIOGRAPHY

Butterick Fashion Marketing Company. Vogue Sewing. New York: Harper & Row, Publishers, 1982.

Shaeffer, Claire. Claire Shaeffer's Fabric Sewing Guide. Radnor, Pennsylvania: Chilton Book Company, 1989.

Jennie Archer Atwood

Jennie Archer Atwood learned to sew as a child from her mother, an accomplished seamstress and prolific maker of doll clothes. Her love of using her hands led her to a Master's degree in Physical Therapy from the University of Iowa. Temporarily retiring to care for her children, the need to complete a task rekindled her love of sewing. Today, using her children as an inspiration and her love of textures as a guide, she designs and creates one-of-kind garments and pillows.

Laura Hotchkiss Brown

Laura Hotchkiss Brown has worked in fashion design for more than 15 years. After training at the Fashion Institute of Technology, she worked as assistant designer to Tracy Mills and Ronaldus Shamask in New York. Laura also teaches at The Sewing Workshop, the Fashion Institute of Design and Merchandising, and Academy of Art College, all in San Francisco. She is a contributing writer to Threads magazine.

Jean Williams Cacicedo

Jean Williams Cacicedo is a nationally renowned fabric artist and a prime innovator in the wearable art movement. Her extraordinary coats incorporating washed and hand-dyed wool and reverse appliqué have been exhibited in galleries and museums throughout the United States and internationally. Jean won a National Endowment for the Arts Crafts Fellowship and was named Artist of the Year by the Oakland Museum in 1985. She maintains her studio and her home in Berkeley, California.

Angela Candela

Angela Candela graduated from Pratt Institute in Brooklyn with a degree in Fashion Design, worked in the garment district in New York, and then moved to San Francisco to work with knitwear designer, Alvin Duskin. For 13 years, she was a pattern designer for Esprit. She began collecting vintage and modern neckties in the 70's, but it wasn't until she moved to Lawrence, Kansas, many years later that she began seriously making one-of-a-kind necktie vests. She enjoys a position as the pattern maker for Asiatica in Kansas City, and she develops patterns for The Sewing Workshop Pattern Collection.

Jean K. Cohen

Jean K. Cohen is a craftsperson who loves to work from scratch in developing an end product. As early as seven years old, she learned to crochet and make doll clothes. Throughout her entire accounting career, she continued to experiment in the needle arts. Her artistry in needlepoint, weaving fabrics for garments, quilting, embroidery, and knitting is well documented and recognized throughout the midwest.

Kathy Davis

Kathy Davis has had an interest in sewing, tailoring, and fabric spanning the last 25 years. She assisted with design development and technical instructions for The Sewing Workshop Pattern Collection and sample making for the <u>Vogue and Butterick's Designer Sewing Techniques</u> book and <u>Sewing Today</u> television series. Trained by The House of Lasage in Paris, Kathy has recently turned her attention to fine hand sewing and embroidery, as well as the book arts.

Dort Johnson

Dort Johnson is known as the "Lady of the Cloth" in Topeka, Kansas. Dort is a self-taught seamstress, learning the hard way, but sewing for the economics of it, for better fit, and for fun. She is the fashion, wardrobe, and fitting consultant at Threadwear, an upscale fabric store. After a life-long career in occupational therapy at the Menninger Foundation and in private practice, she has spent the last eight years producing art (a marriage of art and clay) and volunteering for arts advocacy groups.

Esther Lane

After a long-time career in the insurance business, Esther spent a summer in Atlantic City working and being trained in a professional interior sewing workroom. She returned to Topeka, Kansas, and opened her own business, Lane's Custom Interiors. She specializes in designing and sewing window treatments, slipcovers, upholstery, and accessories with a special expertise in developing unique designs without using a pattern.

Karine Langan

Karine Langan joined The Sewing Workshop as manager in August 1993. She began sewing in 4-H at age 8 and still enjoys sewing for herself and her home. For several years, she had a home decorating consulting business and also was a jewelry buyer for a well-known gift store in San Francisco. Gardening and painting are her hobbies but these days she spends her time at The Sewing Workshop.

Cara Lankard

Cara Lankard is a free-lance graphic artist in Topeka, Kansas. With a BFA in fine arts and post-graduate work in graphic design, she has used her artistic skills to produce a variety of work, including logo design, brochure design, kid's promotional packaging, and all forms of illustration for local and national accounts. She is the illustrator for The Sewing Workshop Pattern Collection.

Kathy Lewis

With degrees in biology and accounting, Kathy uses her analytical skills in her pursuit of sewing excellence. Out of the necessity of having clothes to wear for work and pleasure, she learned to sew in high school and has continued to sew throughout her career as an accountant. Kathy made samples for the PBS sewing series, Sewing Today, the Vogue and Butterick's Designer Sewing Techniques book, and assists in the development of The Sewing Workshop's Pattern Collection. She teaches tailoring and other sewing classes at Threadwear in Topeka, Kansas.

Sherry Nickell

Sherry Nickell is a versatile artist. She is a sculptor whose work incorporates neon tubing in ribbons of light. Her multimedia work is shown in galleries in Kansas City, San Diego, New York, and all over her home state of Kansas. She teaches sculpture and ceramics at Washburn University. Her passion for sewing led her to her current interest in collecting vintage hats and making ribbon hat embellishments and other ribbon arts.

Sharon Ruddy

Sharon Ruddy is a self-taught sewer with a special interest in working with sergers. She was a content contributor and sample maker for the Sewing Today PBS television program and the accompanying book, Vogue & Butterick's Designer Sewing Techniques. Sharon is a factory-trained Bernina technician, sells Bernina sewing machines and sergers, and teaches all levels of serging and sewing classes.

Jo Ann Sutton

Jo Ann's years of collecting antiques and home decorating led her from a 13-year career in the computer industry to her true love — interior design. She is currently owner of Jo Ann Sutton Interiors, Topeka, Kansas, specializing in residential interiors, with emphasis on window and wall treatments. Her particular love of antiques and the Victorian period has led her to collect vintage linens, lace, and trims for many years. Finding new and unique ways to use these old pieces has been an ongoing hobby. She has been involved with many local designer show houses and her work has been published in several national magazines.

Marcy Tilton

Marcy Tilton founded The Sewing Workshop in 1981. She maintains a close bond with The Sewing Workshop, bringing her eclectic inspiring style and classes to San Francisco and other areas. Since her 1993 move to Southern Oregon, she is writing, sewing, developing classes, and making time for gardening, family, and community. Marcy wrote and developed samples for the Vogue & Butterick's Designer Sewing Techniques book, and her book, Easy Guide to Sewing Skirts.

Stephanie Valley

Stephanie Valley's passion for creating and designing led her to a degree in surface design from the University of Kansas. She produces one-of-a-kind silk-screened and hand-stamped fabric yardage and a variety of artistic clothing and accessories. She was the set designer and prop director for the PBS television show, Sewing Today, and is the production director of The Sewing Workshop Pattern Collection. She is the author of Sensational Sachets.

Darchelle Woltkamp

Darchelle Woltkamp is the business manager for The Sewing Workshop in San Francisco and Threadwear in Topeka, Kansas. In addition to her managerial and accounting skills, she is an avid sewer. Her invaluable assistance in the production of The Sewing Workshop Pattern Collection and other special projects is an essential ingredient to the operation of the various business ventures of The Sewing Workshop.

METRIC EQUIVALENTS

Inches to Millimeters and Centimeters
MM - millimeters   CM - centimeters

Inches	MM	CM	Inches	CM	Inches	CM
1/8	3	0.3	9	22.9	30	76.2
1/4	6	0.6	10	25.4	31	78.7
3/8	10	1.0	11	27.9	32	81.3
1/2	13	1.3	12	30.5	33	83.8
5/8	16	1.6	13	33.0	34	86.4
3/4	19	1.9	14	35.6	35	88.9
7/8	22	2.2	15	38.1	36	91.4
1	25	2.5	16	40.6	37	94.0
1 1/4	32	3.2	17	43.2	38	96.5
1 1/2	38	3.8	18	45.7	39	99.1
1 3/4	44	4.4	19	48.3	40	101.6
2	51	5.1	20	50.8	41	104.1
2 1/2	64	6.4	21	53.3	42	106.7
3	76	7.6	22	55.9	43	109.2
3 1/2	89	8.9	23	58.4	44	111.8
4	102	10.2	24	61.0	45	114.3
4 1/2	114	11.4	25	63.5	46	116.8
5	127	12.7	26	66.0	47	119.4
6	152	15.2	27	68.6	48	121.9
7	178	17.8	28	71.1	49	124.5
8	203	20.3	29	73.7	50	127.0

METRIC CONVERSION CHART

Yards	Inches	Meters	Yards	Inches	Meters
1/8	4.5	0.11	1 1/8	40.5	1.03
1/4	9	0.23	1 1/4	45	1.14
3/8	13.5	0.34	1 3/8	49.5	1.26
1/2	18	0.46	1 1/2	54	1.37
5/8	22.5	0.57	1 5/8	58.5	1.49
3/4	27	0.69	1 3/4	63	1.60
7/8	31.5	0.80	1 7/8	67.5	1.71
1	36	0.91	2	72	1.83